MORE TRUTH, LIES & PROPAGAND

By

Lucinda E Clarke

More Truth Lies & Propaganda

Second edition:
Copyright © 2020 Lucinda E Clarke
ISBN 9788409264254
First edition:
Copyright © 2015 Lucinda E Clarke
ISBN 9781508904076

Edited: Andrew Holloway, Fran Macilvey & Zoe Marr
Book cover by Rod Craig & Peter Bendheim
11.12.2020

This is the second and last book about my experiences working in the world of the broadcast and commercial media.

For over 25 years I was privileged to meet hundreds if not thousands of people, who welcomed me into their homes and their lives. They shared their stories with me, some were hilarious, others heartbreakingly sad. I have a deep love for Africa and its peoples of all races and I was so privileged to work with a team of caring and professional people who shared my passion. This book is dedicated to them as a testament to their commitment and belief that we made a small difference in helping to improve lives.

I would like to thank the many fellow authors and readers who have been an inspiration and offered me advice and support. From working in a competitive industry, it has been a revelation to see how both writers and those who enjoy our books help each other and offer encouragement.

Once again I want to acknowledge the enormous debt I owe my husband who has supported me when the computer and I went into hibernation for days on end. I cannot thank him enough for his patience and his love.

Also by Lucinda E Clarke

PSYCHOLOGICAL THRILLER
A Year in the Life of Leah Brand
A Year in the Life of Andrea Coe

FICTION
Amie – an African Adventure
Amie and the Child of Africa
Amie Stolen Future
Amie Cut for Life
Amie Savage Safari
Samantha (Amie backstories)
Ben (Amie backstories)

MEMOIRS
Walking over Eggshells
Truth, Lies and Propaganda
More Truth, Lies and Propaganda
The very Worst Riding School in the World

HUMOUR
Unhappily Ever After

Contents

1   INSPIRATION LOST

Caroline died last night. It was a long, lingering and particularly nasty death - just as I had planned. I had originally decided to kill her by chopping her to pieces under a combine harvester, lots of blood and gore flying everywhere. I could see the birds flying up in protest, small insects bombarded by pieces of her, and the cries of the crowds gathered to stare at the miniscule remains of what had once been a beautiful, young lady. But then at the last minute I changed my mind. Why destroy the peace of the English countryside?

I promised at the end of my last book (*Truth, Lies and Propaganda*) that I would tell you how I finally got rid of Caroline, so I have described her demise at the end of this book.

Are you curious to know what Caroline had done to deserve a vicious and torturous death? Quite frankly I haven't the faintest idea. Perhaps she is the heroine in a book I've not written yet. She is a marvellous example of how you can do exactly what you want to do if you are a writer, as long as you don't put it into practice in everyday life.

As authors we control the lives of those we create, it's one of the perks, but we have a lot less control over our own lives. What was I doing, sitting in a small front room in London, my feet freezing despite the thick woolly socks and furry slippers, my fingers numb as they pecked at the keyboard?

I glanced up at the grey, leaden sky and shivered. I could hear the swish of the cars passing by as their tyres skidded over the wet tarmac and the slap, slap sound from wellington boots as people walked past the house. Years earlier I hadn't even heard of SAD, the syndrome where you get depressed by bad weather and lack of sunshine. Here in London, I had not seen the sun for several days. I remembered my first aeroplane trip when we rose above the clouds, and there, to my amazement, was the sun, throwing its beams over the top of the fluffy white pillows in the sky. It was still there, of course it was! How stupid of me to think the sun had deserted us, but that's the feeling you get when you don't see it for days and days.

What was even worse, this weather was destroying my creativity. I battled to put words on paper, even though I had a contract to write a series of radio programmes for the South African Broadcasting Corporation. (I shall refer to them as the SABC in the future as I'm far too lazy to type it all out each time).

I had recently returned from living in Durban, a city on the east coast of South Africa, fronting the warm Indian Ocean. There, the words flew straight from my brain and magically appeared on the screen, well sort of if you get my drift, I'm using a little poetic licence here.

I began daydreaming about the work I had done in the past, the fun I had with the amazing people I had met. I remembered the excitement of working in the SABC radio studios in Johannesburg, the friends from the Communications Department in Durban and all the wonderful experiences out in the African townships with the crew, while filming a wide variety of programmes.

But that was all over. I had just finished the last SABC programme and I doubted they would ever give me another series, I lived too far away. The classroom beckoned a return to the profession I had trained for decades earlier.

I was not looking forward to it one little bit. I had heard tales of the modern monsters who now inhabited the hallowed halls of learning. If it was bad 30 years before, it was even worse now, 'Health and Safety', and 'I Know My Rights' had seen to that. It seemed to me that a black belt in judo and other martial art qualifications prepared you better for the classroom these days, than the three years they offered you in teacher training college in the 1970s.

What was worse, I was not living in the best area of London either, so I was expecting the worst if they even considered offering me a job. I'd not graced a classroom for years, and I was just a little bit out of touch. No, I was a lot out of touch. The kids would make mincemeat of me.

I had taken the first steps to gainful employment by purchasing, at great cost *'The Writers' and Artists' Yearbook'*, and I had hawked my showreel round every production house listed within commuting distance. I'd received some vague promises for the future, but nothing concrete. If I was honest, there was little chance of me breaking into the broadcast and video industry here. I had been out of the country so long I was totally out of sync with modern Britain.

Looking through my showreel at the short clips we had put together to illustrate some of my work, the people in the production houses were more than underwhelmed, and the general consensus was they liked what they saw, the standard was high, but none of it was relevant to Britain.

Quite frankly, from what I had seen on British television, I was not sure I would fit in. I'd watched teachers get soaked with slime by their pupils in some quiz show, and puppets who spoke English using words I would have slashed through in red pen, or instantly corrected if used by my own children. A few programmes I couldn't understand at all, and I was forced to activate the subtitles for the deaf, because the dialogue was so indistinct or the accents too broad.

Other programmes made dozens of references to people, events and ideas I had never heard of. Also, the majority of the television offerings seemed so hyped up, they sounded like the commentary on the 'Grand National' horse race, and that wasn't my style at all.

I also cringed at the one-sided documentaries shown on British television. I had learned my lesson about that, years ago, with my ideas about acupuncture in animals, where I had simply refused to produce a programme showing both sides of the story. It never got made.

The closest I came to getting any work was a vague promise of a script on surgical gloves from an outfit based at Shepperton Studios, and then only because the producer had African connections. I'd written about stranger things in the past, but it was hardly a subject to get wildly excited about. Not only that, it *might* come off in four months time. I wasn't sure I could manage without food for that long.

I had tried for dozens of other jobs. I applied for anything that was on offer. The supermarkets didn't want me working on their tills, not very surprising as I was still peering at the coins trying to figure out what they were worth. The local pub turned me down, I obviously wouldn't have a clue as to what I was doing, even the teaching establishment which had trained me did not seem keen to put me back on the register. I even had trouble understanding the various British accents. People would talk to me and I wouldn't have the faintest idea what they were saying.

No one wanted me, not even the Labour Exchange, or Job Centre or whatever they called it these days. I walked in to sign on and sat down opposite a girl almost young enough to be my daughter.

"So, I see from this form you have been living outside Britain?" She waved my completed form like a flag.

"Yes."

"In another country?"

"Yes."

"Where was it? Not in Britain then?"

"No."

"So you have not been working in Britain then?"

I thought that was just a teeny bit obvious, but I replied politely, "No, I was working in Africa, South Africa." Then I added in the hope of really impressing her "I've always worked, I even took my youngest daughter into the classroom in her carry cot."

If I thought this would either impress her, or prove I was a hard working individual it failed. She gave me a horrified glare before reluctantly lowering her eyes again to the form on her desk.

"Out of the country then for..." The young girl on the other side of the desk began calculating the time I'd spent away.

Finally she had got it! I had been out of the country, overseas, not in Britain, abroad, in exile, not domiciled in the United Kingdom, the other side of the Channel, in a foreign land. The Monty Python parrot sketch flashed before my eyes.

"Just over 20 years." I was trying to be helpful.

"I can count," she snapped back, and went on reading the form I thought I had filled in very neatly.

"Hmmm, and you think you can just walk back in and claim unemployment benefit I suppose?" she said with a sneer. I thought this was a little unfair, since I suspected her ancestors had originally come from much warmer climes.

"No! I've not come to ask for money, I just wanted to get back into the system and have my stamps credited." Actually that was a big fat lie, I most certainly did *not* want to get back in the system, I didn't want to be back here at all, but here I was and here I was likely to stay. There was a future pension to think about.

She looked up and gave me a withering look. "We don't have stamps anymore," she sniffed.

"Oh, well whatever you have now then. I will be looking for work." I fought back my instinct to pass her a handkerchief.

"That's nice to hear, since you've paid nothing into the system while you've been away." She made it sound as if I had just been released from a psychiatric unit or a long term prison sentence.

"I'll need your bank account details," she snapped.

"You do? What for?" I asked.

She looked at me and I could see the pity, or was it contempt, in her eyes I wasn't sure which.

"So we can send you your money."

"But I thought I said, uh, you said..." I was becoming confused.

"Look," she said slowly, as if talking to a deranged three year old, "if you are entitled to money then we have to pay you. It's your right." The last word flew out of her mouth like a bullet and she turned and tapped away on her keyboard. "It appears you are in the system, so you will be getting a cheque in..." she paused to exercise her limited maths ability, "... two weeks time. It will have to last until the next one. We pay out every other week. So what's your bank account number?"

I had to think hard about that. I only had one account in Britain, if you ignore the one we'd left in the red all those years ago. I had opened another one from South Africa a couple of years ago to accept the royalty cheques from my first book. I'd hoped they would flood in at regular intervals, paid by the publisher's head office in London. No such luck, as far as I knew it still held the princely sum of £4.10. I gave her the details and watched as she sniffed her way through the rest of the paperwork.

Welcome home, I thought as I fled the government offices after my protracted and painful interview. Nice to know they are thrilled to see you back in your native country. What a lovely warm welcome that was.

The doorbell rang, bringing me back from my daydream, and the front door opened and closed. There was a brief knock on the inner door.

"Come in," I cried, "I won't be a moment, it's almost ready."

"I can wait, don't rush," said a voice with a broad Cockney accent.

I slid the scripts with the covering letter into a large envelope and turned to hand it to the courier.

"Good heavens, you're black!"

The courier looked most alarmed and took an involuntary step backwards.

"Oh, look, I'm so sorry," I mumbled, "I didn't mean to be rude in any way, it's just that..." How could I explain that, where I had been for so many years, the *African* people spoke with a distinctly *African* accent? Here was another British person whose ancestors had come from a far-off land but who had been born and raised in Britain and sounded utterly British.

"Sorry," I muttered. "Uh, I've only just recently returned from Africa. You surprised me, that's all."

The courier smiled. "No offence," he said.

"And this," I indicated the envelope, "is on its way to Johannesburg."

"That's in Africa?"

"Yes, South Africa."

"Never been to Africa," the courier replied.

"It's a wonderful continent," I replied, "and I miss it."

"Then we've sort of swapped places," the courier said as he placed my envelope inside his company package, tore off the perforated strip and handed it to me. "You going back there?"

"I wish, maybe. I want to, but I'm not sure I can."

But wait a minute! What was stopping me? Apart from money, what *was* stopping me? I was unhappy here in London. I missed the bright blue skies, the feeling of drum beats under my feet pulsing up from the vibrant, dusty soil, and the almost palpable feeling of underlying danger which kept me feeling alive, alert, and constantly on my toes.

Only the night before, my youngest daughter had told me how unhappy she was in England. She missed the discipline of her school in Durban, she had been shocked by the sight of drugs in her British school, and she was no longer studying subjects like maths and geography. She missed her friends too. She wanted to finish her secondary schooling 'properly' and get her matriculation exam, which she had been due to take in another eighteen months.

Maybe it didn't have to be a permanent return. If I could get some work, the work I loved, then I could earn enough to keep us both while she finished studying.

A moment later, my fingers were flying over the keyboard, composing a message to the studio in Durban. If I returned, could they find work for me? I read it through once, before I pushed it into the fax machine and pressed the send button.

The reply came back within minutes.

"Get on the next plane, we will make it happen. Welcome back!" As I read it, my eyes filled with tears. I wanted so much to go back, not only to the country I loved but to the work I adored. The die was cast. I had very little money and nowhere to live in Durban but somehow I would cope.

I was like a fish out of water here in Britain, and life is too short to accept what makes you unhappy. The decision was made. My youngest daughter and I would return to KwaZulu-Natal.

My husband declined the invitation to come with us. He made it quite clear he would never, ever, set foot on African soil again.

2   A VANISHING HOUSE & DEAD BODIES

As the plane banked over Jan Smuts Airport in Johannesburg I looked out of the window, half expecting to see signs of riots, battles, civil unrest of some kind, maybe blood flowing everywhere? But no, it all looked peaceful.

The British media were speculating on the troubles that would break out as the first democratic elections approached, almost as if they *hoped* there would be pitched battles in the streets to make exciting copy for their newspapers and television screens. It was early April in 1994.

We were greeted with big smiles, offers to help with luggage, and a cheerful, friendly atmosphere, as we weaved our way through the crowds to the domestic departures. We had one more hop to go, an hour's internal flight, to reach Durban.

We were met at the airport by our old friends, and we spent a couple of days with them while I looked for somewhere to live. Previously I had lived on a boat in Durban harbour, but I had sold that before leaving. She was still there, floating on the water, but she did not belong to me anymore. I would have to find somewhere else to live, and quickly.

I scoured the papers the moment they came off the press, you had to be quick off the mark as decent flats were snapped up in no time. It was only by chance a friend, who also lived on a boat in the harbour, was the night editor on the local paper. He tipped me off there was a vacant flat in town in my price range, that was close to rock bottom. The advert would be out in the morning.

Yes it was small, and dark, and right on the Victoria Embankment, a popular route for police cars in hot pursuit of criminals, and ambulances on their way to the hospital. So it certainly wasn't quiet. While the front of the art deco, listed building faced the harbour, our flat faced a side street overlooking offices where the employees never switched their computers off. Every night I could watch their screen savers as they flitted up and down the monitors and I could also look down on the drunks as they weaved their way across the road to sleep in the public toilets at the entrance to the yacht mole. You can tell it was a really upmarket area.

However, it was central and I could walk to the studio, and it was on the bus route that passed the high school. My daughter and I would have to share the one and only bedroom, but it was fully furnished and we could move in right away.

It did not take long for us to settle back into our previous routine, only this time we did not have to catch the ferry to and from the boat, and I didn't have to panic each time the weather forecasters said there were storms and strong winds on the horizon. We were now firmly settled on dry land.

By the time I had handed over the deposit and the first

month's rent to the greasy Greek landlord who lived next door, I was all but broke. I didn't know it at the time, but the 'Greasy Greek' was to become the bane of my life. He was always knocking on my front door saying he had come to un-bung my drains. They were not bunged up, I would tell him, but that was no excuse. He would sweep past me, plunger in hand and attack the plug hole in the kitchen sink. Sometimes he would vary this and make for the plug holes in the bathroom instead.

I kept my distance, mostly to avoid the smell of the sweat coming from his armpits and the overwhelming aura of garlic that floated in the air behind him. His favourite outfit was a string vest, which tried in vain to contain the long grey chest hair which poked through the holes, while the rest of him inhabited a pair of dirty grey trousers tied around his waist with string.

After several unnecessary visits un-bunging plug holes that were not bunged up, I got brave and refused to let him in. As long as I paid the rent on time, it was all he was entitled to as far as I was concerned. I was not offering my body along with the rand notes at the end of each month. The thought of running my fingers through his matted, greasy hair was enough to put me off sex for life.

I took to scuttling through the front door on my way in and out, and over to the rubbish chute. I shamelessly used my daughter as a living shield and tried to co-ordinate our exits and entrances at the same time. It was exhausting. As soon as I had a few cents in the bank, I vowed to move at the earliest opportunity.

It felt strange walking into the studio the first morning.

The last time I had walked out, it was after my leaving party, clutching my presents and card with best wishes from all the staff. Now, three months later, here I was again and it was a little surreal.

But nothing had changed, except the scriptwriter they had engaged in the meantime. Luckily he had also been employed on a freelance basis, but I felt very guilty that now he would probably lose his job. After all the 'welcome back' and 'how was England?' comments were over, we got down to business. I was told to sit down for a chat about the next programme they were planning.

"You are never going to believe this," said Brian, who was in charge of the studio and did most of the editing.

"You are never going to believe this," he repeated, "but the Housing Department want to show people how to build a better squatter house."

"You can't be serious, this is some sort of 'welcoming back' joke isn't it?"

"No! Despite the recent floods and fires in the settlements, they know they can't stop people moving into town. But the new migrants are putting up such awful shacks they are falling down almost immediately."

"So, run that by me again, they want to show what?"

"They want to explain how to build a dwelling that is more substantial than the packing case shacks that are going up now."

"I've heard that one Toyota car parts packing crate is now going for R5,000," remarked Carl, the cameraman.

"You're kidding!" I was shocked, that was the price of a slap-up dinner for four at a top London restaurant. "I don't believe that for one moment."

"I had heard they weren't cheap," Brian agreed. "Anyhow, after much discussion and research, it's generally been decided that the more traditional ways of building houses are the best."

"If this is for real, I think there's only one way to really prove that, and convince the audience at the same time," I added.

"What's that?"

"We actually build one." Both guys looked at me in horror. "No, I don't mean *we* build it but we get the council workers to put one up and we have the usual dramatised story containing all those subliminal hidden messages we drive home with a sledgehammer."

"That's a relief," Carl said. He loved his work behind the camera, his fishing, his car, and cute babes, but he was not into house building.

Before I go any further and in case you have not read the first part of my memoirs about working in the media, perhaps a bit of background might help put you in the picture.

I began working in radio when I was living in Benghazi in Libya then, years later, when I was living outside Johannesburg in South Africa, circumstances brought me into contact with the SABC. I did warn you that I wouldn't be writing out the South African Broadcasting Corporation every time didn't I? Bother, I just have.

I had many interesting experiences over the following years but, after suffering burn-out twice, the new plan for the family was to live on the partly-purchased boat moored in Durban harbour. After a year, we would sail away to explore the world. In the meantime I was going to quickly become a best-selling novelist, which would also fund our travels over the ocean waves.

We must have been out of our minds! (No, we *were* out of our minds.) All that happened was that after the first housekeeping cheque bounced the children began to whine they were starving to death. Strange they should mention that, I was getting a bit hungry as well. I needed to get work in Durban urgently

By chance I met up with the guys who worked in the Durban Municipal Communications Video Unit, one of the few such departments in South Africa and, I suspect, anywhere in the world. But then Durban was a very special city. Way back when the swampland was first drained, and the sandbar to the harbour entrance was dredged, the city fathers had the foresight to buy up the land surrounding the harbour and bay. In time they became the major landlords for what was to become a vibrant, commercial centre.

I had been freelancing for the Communications Department for a couple of years before my brief sojourn in England. Finally and with a great sense of coming home, I was back, ready to write the script for 'How to Build a Better Squatter House', a bit of a cosmic joke given my own housing situation. You couldn't make it up, honestly!

All over South Africa government departments were throwing up thousands of what were called RDP (Reconstruction and Development Plan) houses, cheap and nasty boxes made of powdery, grey breeze blocks, topped off with a corrugated tin roof, which were freezing cold in winter and boiling hot in summer. Now the Durban

Council, in its wisdom, had the sense to see that the original African *rondavels*, (huts made of mud mixed with cow dung and topped with a thatched roof) were ideal for the African climate.

Sadly nowadays, traditional round houses are not seen as being modern and upmarket, but maybe in our programme we could suggest ways of making a temporary house much safer?

New arrivals to the city seldom had much money and they would construct a lean-to shelter with whatever materials they could find. Often these shelters were both health and fire hazards. After extensive research, the Housing Department came up with a method of building that included the use of traditional materials with low-cost additions. Since cow dung was a little thin on the ground in the city, the Housing Department had experimented with a liquid which, when added to the mud worked almost as well as cow dung, and it smelt a lot nicer too.

I wrote a comedy script around a lazy city dweller, showing off to his relatives who had just moved into town, telling them how to construct this superior house. He didn't actually work, he only pretended to, while conning the rest of the cast into doing all the manual labouring.

We were using employees from the Housing and Health Departments to act the parts, but the truth was that while we shot a little of the action each day with them, another team of council workers would move in later and build a little more. To save time and cost we were only planning on a two-sided house, as we could shoot from various angles and cheat a little. Ok, we were going to cheat a lot!

The shoot was going very well. The cast was really excellent and we didn't even need to understand the words spoken in Zulu, their actions made the messages crystal clear. We had done so well that, by Friday night when we packed away, I thought we should be able to wrap the whole thing in another day and a half. I looked forward to a relaxing weekend.

We arrived bright and early on the following Monday morning and, for a brief moment, I thought I was hallucinating. I went into a mild state of shock and grabbed my cell (mobile) phone. While I called the Housing Department, Carl phoned the studio.

"We've lost our house!"

"What do you mean you've lost the house? You can't lose a house."

"Well we have. When we left on Friday night, it was almost complete. Now it's gone, not a post, not a brick, not a wall in sight, it's just bare earth! The house is gone, it's not there anymore. I've got six actors down here wandering around looking for their set." I just knew I was never going to live this down it's not every day you lose a house.

It transpired that the Civil Protection patrols had seen our 'set' and, because we were building in an unsuitable area (it was on a flood plain), they followed their orders and demolished what they saw as an illegal build. I was not comforted by the report they showed me, which stated that:

'The half-completed structure was particularly difficult to destroy, as it had been extremely well built and resisted our initial attempts to demolish it.'

So what were we going to do? The only answer was to build and film another house, right from scratch, as the continuity would have been a nightmare between the first house and the second. They would not look the same. After showing the programme in all the informal settlements, Durban should have been able to boast the best built squatter houses in South Africa!

However, I have to admit that I never saw one traditional-type house built in an informal settlement, despite visiting many in the months that followed, so maybe no one followed the examples we set in the programme. But perhaps they had a good laugh and were entertained for a while.

The Parks and Gardens Department were among my favourite clients. The Botanical Gardens were extremely old, beautifully maintained and, I was amazed to learn, had provided Kew Gardens in London with many samples over the last couple of hundred years.

We had made several programmes for them in the past, including one which was part of the package for an international competition for the best 'City in Bloom'. We had used a young schoolgirl as a presenter, and she took us on a tour of 'her' town and explained why she loved it, not only for the beauty of its parks and gardens but also for its environmental practices. We understood that our video would play a major part of the presentation.

I believe Durban came second that year, but they might not have got the award if the judges had realised the truth behind the hanging baskets which adorned the main city streets. Now these had been around for years, beautiful pink, yellow and red flowers cascading from the lamp posts, but then the vandals moved in. As fast as the city replaced the baskets, they were either stolen or destroyed.

This next bit is very sad. Pride of place in the Botanical Gardens is the last remaining natural *Wood's Cycad*, but it is a male and, since not one female plant is left anywhere on the planet, it is destined to be the last of its kind. There are a few clones in other specialised gardens but this is the real one taken from the oNgoye forest in KwaZulu-Natal. There it stands all by itself in a quiet corner of the garden. It will never again propagate and its days are numbered.

So when it came to filming, we had to wait until the Parks personnel had hung up a row of baskets, capture this on video, and then wait while they took them all down, raced round the corner and put the same flowers up on another row of lamp posts for us to shoot, and so on.

As we packed away the camera, the flowers were already in the van on their way back to the municipal nurseries. It wasn't really cheating I guess, but it was depressing to think that, unguarded, these flowers would not live to bloom another day.

A great innovation was the cultivation of medicinal herbs and other plants. For someone who can hardly tell a daisy from a dandelion I was fascinated by all the weird and wonderful shrubs they showed us.

Traditional medicine is still alive and well in Africa, and many of the remedies used in these ancient traditions are beneficial, as I was to discover a couple of years later. On the outskirts of Durban's central business district there are several '*muti*' (traditional medicine) shops where you could purchase all kinds of stuff, from a shrunken monkey's head, to a desiccated lion's paw, to unspecified powders and dried plants.

With Durban's population growing daily, the plant gatherers now had to travel further and further away to find medicinal plants, until the council nursery hit on the idea of growing them in the greenhouses right in the city.

However, I was feeling quite cheerful on the day I was called in to collect the information for another programme the Parks people wanted the video unit to make. It was the first time I had met the new head of department, a charming African who offered me coffee as we settled down to talk.

"Durban is running out of space," he began.

I found this very hard to believe. You only had to travel for five minutes in the car and you were out in the countryside, with miles and miles of rolling hills on every side, except the side next to the sea.

He saw my face and smiled. "Yes, I know it looks as if there is plenty of open, vacant land out there, but let's remove all the areas where the informal settlements are, the vast number of acres which are under sugar cane, and all the market gardens owned and run by the Indian population, and there is not so much left."

I could see his point. "So what does your department need more land for?" I asked. There was no space in the city to extend the Botanical Gardens.

"Burying dead people," he replied, much to my astonishment. "While an open piece of land might look suitable for burials, there are all kinds of factors involved, such as ground water seepage, flooding, soil erosion and so on. Also much of the land around Durban is already zoned for future development and in many places the terrain is no use for cemeteries."

I nodded and tried to look convinced. It had never occurred to me that you might have to do a feasibility study to discover where you were going to bury bodies. Surely people throughout history simply dug holes anywhere it was convenient? Not for the first time, I realised that there was so much I didn't know.

"I'm not quite sure what, uh, how we can...?" I was lost for words.

"Durban is hosting the *International Cemeteries Conference* and we want to show a video on how we intend to change mindsets."

"About what?" I was now totally puzzled, but the manager went on to explain, and in the next hour I was amazed as he told me the problems they had.

The worst was probably the noisy and unruly mobs of mourners attending the weekend funerals, who dropped litter and had parties in the graveyards. If the deceased happened to be a car hijacker by profession, a new tradition involved stealing a car and then setting fire to it, while the nearest and dearest of the lately deceased fired guns by the graveside.

I'll divert here for a moment to share an urban legend I am assured is true. Two men hijacked a car early one morning, forcing the driver at gunpoint to drive them out of the city. Suddenly, one of the men mentioned that the car was a 'black' BMW. They asked the driver what colour his car was and he confirmed it was black.

"Stop the car!" shrieked one of the hijackers, checking

the list he brought out of his pocket. "We don't want this one, the order's for a dark blue one."

The driver skidded to a halt, the hijackers jumped out, apologised for the inconvenience and walked off.

Back to the cemeteries, where another tradition involved digging sideways at the bottom of the hole to prevent the spirits escaping or, if that was not possible because it was right next to another grave, they covered the coffin with large quantities of cement. It sounded as if dying was a dangerous business, for the cemetery staff in particular, and any other mourners who happened to be close by.

Weekends were incredibly busy, as several dozen funerals were held within a few hours, so I was relieved to know that we would be shooting, only with the camera, during the week. I was later to learn that a funeral was an opportunity for a day out, and people who had never even heard of the newly deceased would get all dressed up, gatecrash the party, and make a beeline for the free food and drink afterwards. The Africans do love to party.

"I can understand all the problems," I said, "but do you have any answers?"

"One is to try and persuade people to book funerals during the week."

"Right, we'll include that." I scribbled in my notebook.

"We want you to say that the first payment for a grave is only for 25 years, and if it's not paid for again after that time, we have decided to re-use that grave for someone else."

I added that to the list as well. "But don't the Africans often visit graves to commune with their ancestors?" I was a bit shocked at the thought of recycling them and I couldn't see many Africans agreeing to that.

"Maybe in the beginning, but we've noticed that after a couple of years in this modern day and age, they are generally ignored and no one visits the graves," our client said. "I have a few fact sheets here with more information."

I stood up to go. "That's sounds fine, I should be able to have the first draft..." Before I could finish he interrupted me.

"That's not all. The main purpose of the video - we want you to strongly suggest that people consider cremation."

My mouth fell open and I fell rather than sat back down. It's *never* been part of the African tradition to cremate the dead. The burial rituals are quite rigid, and ancestor worship or, at the least, communication with those who have gone before was still a fundamental belief. Often, when believers changed churches, they took their ancestors with them and they were all baptised into the new faith with the living representing their deceased family members at a second or even third baptism. Surely no one was going to believe they could communicate with their late family members if they'd been reduced to ashes. This was a radical attempt to change mindsets.

"Do you know of any Africans who have been cremated?"

"One."

"One? Would it be possible to interview any of the family on camera?"

"We can try and set it up for you."

It didn't dawn on me, until I walked back into the studio, that there was another problem. Except for Brian and Carl, the rest of the crew who were in permanent employment with the municipality were black Africans and when I told them the purpose of the programme they were aghast.

The second cameraman Subisiso was very unhappy, and I was not sure if he was going to agree to go along with it.

I personally thought we would have a hard time convincing any audience there was no space for more burial grounds. You only had to look at the rolling green hills around the city. We could explain that it wasn't possible to use the land planted with sugar cane, referred to locally as 'green gold'.

In the past the newly arrived farmers had tried every crop they could think of to grow in Natal, to the extent it was called 'T*he Province of Trials*'. It was only when they tried planting sugar cane that the economy really took off.

I knew neither the script nor the shoot was going to be easy, and I could forget my usual comedy routine this time. Death is a serious business and punting cremation might well be positively dangerous.

It's also a very difficult job to persuade people to accept new ideas on the strength of preserving the environment for future generations, which was one of the points the client wanted us to make. Too many people were far too busy trying to survive day to day in the present to worry about the state of the land hundreds of years down the road.

The only positive point in cremation I could see was

the cost. I first arranged to interview Hindu and Christian leaders and we mentioned the financial advantages of cremation, time and time again throughout the script.

The only black African lady who'd had her father cremated also declared loudly that it was so much cheaper, but I suspected her choice of disposal was partly based on revenge for some action of his in the past. She seemed to take great delight in telling us her father would have not approved and would have turned in his grave, if he'd had one. After stating this fact at full volume, she began to cackle very loudly and then burst into a fit of hysterical laughter. I made sure that bit was edited out, as I didn't think it conveyed quite the right message.

We spent six days shooting in the cemeteries, recording how the cremation chambers worked and watching how they cleared out the ashes afterwards and brushed them into jam jars before popping those into brown paper bags.

All the time I was looking over my shoulder, hoping and praying that a well known heroic hijacker was not making his last journey in our direction. I'd thrown myself flat on the ground too many times in the past to avoid imaginary hails of bullets, usually to the enjoyment of the rest of the crew.

We were all highly amused at the tales of some families, who the moment the coffin dropped out of sight, raced with indecent speed down below to stand and watch until it had been loaded into the ovens. They wanted to make quite sure the coffin, with all its handles and decorations, went into the ovens intact, so no part of it could be recycled. They had paid good money for the very best caskets for their loved ones and they were not going to be cheated, to subsidise another family or enrich the funeral parlour.

But I could tell that Subisiso the cameraman and Shezi, who always assisted us, were not happy working on this shoot. The idea was contrary to their beliefs, and it was an uncomfortable few days as we wandered around cemeteries, filming the plaques on the *wall of remembrance,* and interviewing people in the streets looking for anyone who would agree with not only cremation but attending funerals during the week.

I don't know how successful the video was, or what reception it had at the conference, but I do know that the council were actively recycling graves in Durban's oldest cemetery, as I saw a small excavator in there a couple of weeks later.

Since Durban is a coastal city, it's at risk of flooding and twice in the 16 years that I lived there, many of the roads became impassable. They have even installed pumps in the basement of the theatre which switch on automatically at high tide to keep the water levels under control.

The Environmental Department of the Council was very active and one of their managers was frequently invited to address international conferences, especially for the *LA 21* initiative which formulates sustainability across the world.

We made several videos for her to help illustrate her presentations, and I remember one in particular as it featured global warming. Why do I remember it?

Well, there were some great graphics in it which showed how the rise in the levels of the oceans, due to the melting of the polar ice caps and other factors, would affect Durban. The problem was the figures for the exact rise in the sea levels seemed to change on a daily basis. I have no idea where they came from, maybe several of the research institutes scattered across the globe came up with different statistics, but I do know that those graphics were changed 35 times before the programme was finally accepted.

If the forecasters are right, in the future, large areas of Durban will be below sea level. The city isn't knee deep in water yet, but thousands of semi-formal houses have sprung up in the various squatter camps around the perimeter. As the population climbed to over two million, Durban was declared a Metro, or megacity. The city had to celebrate this of course, another great excuse for a party and free nibbles! I'm not sure if every South African town was the same, but even the slightest reason was a good excuse to plan a get-together, dress up and scoff free food and drink, along with various speeches and entertainment. I will have to admit here that such events were yet another opportunity for the political leaders to spout their rhetoric for hours and hours on end.

While I was still writing speeches for the mayor, I tried to keep these as short as possible, and also inclusive, basing my content on the 'let's pull together' theme used by Nelson Mandela. Too often our mayor would wander away from the point, let my carefully crafted words fall to the floor and 'speak from the heart'. Then we knew we were in for a long, long, very long session.

But Africans do like to talk and talk and talk (and this is probably the reason why there is better cell phone coverage there than in many other countries). The speeches on all these celebratory occasions could last for ages, which only went to prove the truth of the saying; 'There is no such thing as a free lunch.'

With a population of over two million people, Durban has a large industrial base and is one of the largest centres for the manufacture of chemicals, a by-product of which is the sale of those large 45 gallon drums. These are really useful in both the urban and rural areas, but after 35 children died from contact with contaminated drums, the council needed to take action to prevent the stealing and resale of untreated containers.

Many people were happy to buy cheap drums, usually those containers that had *'climbed over the fence and fallen down on the outside of the facility'* - where they should have been properly cleaned and sanitised. Most people thought that a quick rinse in the river would make them safe to use. How many of us would even think of using a dirty chemical drum to store beer or fruit drinks? We would be much too scared. It was another case of educating people who were simply unaware of the dangers and making them conscious that saving a few cents could invite certain death.

Our programme told the story of a man who often collected commercially cleaned, safe drums for sale in the local market, but then he agreed to collect some containers at night, through a hole in the factory fence and use forged papers to pass the inspectors at the market. He was desperate for extra money to pay for his daughter's wedding. Unbeknown to him, his wife bought two of the drums and served beer and fruit juice to the wedding guests. As a result, two days after the wedding the man was attending his daughter's funeral. No happy Hollywood ending, this was a serious programme with a serious message.

There were no further incidents reported in the press, but that is not to say our message was one hundred per cent successful. People could still die as a result of being cursed by the local *sangoma* (witch doctor), and I'm honestly not sure if autopsies were performed on all sudden deaths in and around the city. There were probably far too many of them.

I do remember on that shoot I had written in a couple of shots of the mortuary. At the time, I reasoned a quick picture of the exterior would be quite good enough, but the client thought this was a 'really good' message to get across and was eager for us to go inside. Yes! Inside! He wanted scenes inside the mortuary! Well I've done some stupid things in my time, but writing myself into a mortuary scene must be one of the dumbest.

If we had been one of those large Hollywood film crews I might have been able to slide away unnoticed into the background but, when you are one of only three crew members, your absence is just a tad more obvious. As a Director, which is a very smart term for me waving my arms about telling either Subisiso or Carl what to film (in Carl's case it was more telling him what *not* to film), if I wasn't there, someone would notice.

"No, we do not need any shots of those cute babes on the beach with hardly any clothes, we're shooting a programme on the sewer system so I need a shot down that open manhole into the drains. Right Carl? Not such an exciting shot I admit, but we are explaining waste water here, not half naked women."

Five minutes later, "No Carl, I am not going to ask that cute babe to come and stand next to the open manhole while you shoot. Now why on earth would she be standing next to an open manhole cover in the first place? Don't you agree that would look just a little unrealistic?"

So there we were, Carl and Shezi, with me cowering behind them, walking ever so slowly into the mortuary. First the smell hit us, some sort of chemical, something I had never noticed when watching CSI.

There were several sad looking people hanging about, I could only think they were there to identify recently departed loved ones, as everyone else was attired in green gowns, masks and matching green bootees. Even Carl had stopped fantasising about his cute babes. This was serious stuff.

I really didn't think we needed to shoot much, just enough to cover two short sentences. Time the length of the sentences, fifteen seconds, allow three seconds per shot, that makes five shots, but if I include a five second pan, that cuts it down to two extra shots, maybe even a quick pan inside as well, from left to right, and we were out of there. Good, let's get going.

I had forgotten about the enthusiasm of our hosts. It was not often that television cameras poked their lens through the front doors of the mortuary, and they were oh so keen to show us *everything*. The trick now was to follow the guided tour, with my eyes firmly closed, without falling over anything gruesome.

"Just get me the two shots and the pan and let's get out of here, but whatever you do, don't show any dead faces, and no tags hanging off the toes either," I hissed in Carl's ear. "Just a couple of green clad humps on trolleys and a wide shot of the fridge doors should do it, and then we leg it."

Shezi was as stalwart as always. Just as he never turned a hair during that appalling plane ride, (recounted in the first book), the presence of dead bodies did not faze him in the slightest. It must have been all that slaughtering of the animals on feast days when he was growing up in his rural village.

In comparison, we are real hypocrites and weaklings when it comes to real life. I'd said many times I am only a carnivore if someone else does all the nasty, 'behind the scenes' stuff. If I thought this was, bad I didn't know what was still in store for me in the future!

3 CATALYST FOR MURDER

I admit I've only ever worked for one city council, but I think ours had a particularly vibrant video department. We were busy making one programme after another. We always tried to make the information lively and interesting with 'fable type' stories that would entertain. We covered such diverse topics as *'Why You Needed to Pay Rates'* and *'What Your Rates Money Is Used For'*.

There were many instances when the new middle-class black society bought houses, and then were astounded to find that they had to pay more money each month just to live in them. Many refused, as they felt this situation was totally unjust, and I'm talking about apparently well educated professional people, such as lawyers, doctors and professors who had educational certificates coming out of their ears.

I guess it all comes down to the expectations you grow up with. For example on one shoot in the *Valley of a Thousand Hills*, I was talking to one of the local chiefs and he offered me a piece of land. Naturally *I* didn't take him too seriously, but *he* was serious and apparently he had every right to offer it to me.

There was a catch of course, there always is. As the overlord, he had the authority to say who he would allow to live within his area. If permitted, it was up to the incumbent to construct a dwelling, assuming there wasn't one there already.

But, as you give, you can also take away, and if I had taken him up on his offer, and then built a house, I could expect him to come and reclaim it whenever he fancied. So, upset your Chief and you can be without a roof over your head in short order, which must be very difficult for the local people who can never feel totally secure in their own homes.

Thinking about it later, something my maid said to me when we were still back in Johannesburg made sense. I had asked her if she had made up her mind which party she was going to vote for in the next elections. I didn't want her to tell me the name of the candidate she would vote for, just if she had made a decision.

Her reply was that when she went home at the weekend she would ask her Chief and he would tell her who to vote for. It has been very hard to persuade some new voters in South Africa the ballot is secret and no one would know who you choose. They are convinced that some unearthly being will be cowering over the curtained booth waiting to report back on their actions.

After my conversation with this Chief, suddenly Agnes' reply made sense. Later I asked Shezi how he felt about having a family home without any long term security, but he just smiled and shrugged. As a full time employee of the council, he was now eligible for a low interest home loan and with great enthusiasm he applied for one and was soon off to find a house to buy.

Luckily Brian was able to dissuade him from purchasing his first choice, as the papers were not in order, and the house didn't even belong to the seller. The second time round, Shezi decided on a dwelling that was legally for sale, and with great pride he moved himself and a couple of his wives in, with a few of his children, and all went well.

However it must have been about twelve months later when he took me to one side and asked for help.

"What's the problem?"

"It's my house, something is wrong, look." He handed me a statement from the bank showing his monthly bond (mortgage) payments, and pointed to the totals.

"See. I have paid all this money," he ran his finger down the figures, "but here it says I still owe all this on the house. Are they trying to cheat me?"

With maths never being a particular accomplishment, I puzzled as to how I was going to even begin to explain how and why homeowners paid off the interest on house loans first on a sliding scale, with only a few cents being deducted from the principal capital at the start of the loan. As I tried to explain this, drawing lots of little diagrams on paper, showing the variations in compound interest and all the other ramifications, I could see I was not getting through.

Twenty minutes later, we were knee deep in scribbled diagrams and charts and little pictures, when Shezi grabbed my arm and said:

"I would be better going back to my village and sitting outside my house all day and not worrying about things like this. Why am I working so hard? It is all for nothing!" Grabbing the papers he walked off to the kitchen muttering to himself.

He did have a point. It put a whole new perspective on our way of life. We were encouraging people to transfer their lives into what we call the 'first world', acquiring material possessions together with all the monthly bills, when many of them were, for the most part, happy in the old world.

I don't know what happened to Shezi's house, nor to his family, although I was invited there once and met many of them. Sadly, a few years later he died. I will always remember him with great fondness.

Although much of the land around Durban is owned by one local Chief or another there is also the *Ingonyama Trust*. This is land traditionally owned and run by the Zulu king, the premier of the provincial government and the House of the Traditional Leaders. In total it owns and manages the mineral rights to three million hectares, or thirty two per cent of the land area, which is home to over four million people.

This makes life difficult for the Durban City Council, since the Trust does not pay taxes to the municipality. As a result, many of the recipients of the upliftment schemes on the outskirts of the city, which fall inside the borders of the Trust, see no reason to pay, for improvements, or for services.

This did not stop the council from doing their best and working flat out to build more homes and supply each one with power, water and sanitation. It was an ongoing project and, as fast as they had the money to build, the population explosion continued to grow in leaps and bounds.

Education was the key to changing mindsets and

bridging the gap between the old and the new world, and that is where we came in. If we could make videos that entertained and taught at the same time, we might help to make a difference.

A good example was the education information centre that Durban Solid Waste (DSW) set up at their largest landfill site, which was visited by parties of school children. They would watch our programmes which explained how waste was collected, how it was sorted and then disposed of.

I spent many afternoons standing on piles of rubbish trying not to sink in too deeply. Those huge rubbish piles might look solid and closely packed, but you have to keep moving or, like quicksand, you find yourself slowly being sucked down among the tin cans, bottles, rotting food, used nappies and other indescribable stuff I simply can't mention here. I went through more than one pair of shoes and boots which were sometimes just not salvageable after a day spent leaping around in discarded household trash. That puts a different perspective on the glamour and magic of filming doesn't it?

If we looked over to the far end of the main dump, which covered a vast area, we could see the people who had climbed in through a hole they had cut in the fence. They were rummaging around looking for discarded food, or anything else they could find a use for.

DSW also had several innovative schemes not just for recycling the rubbish, but making it pay for itself. Large sheets of plastic were laid to protect the underlying soil, and methane was collected to be converted into electricity and fed into the national grid.

I thought I had a very bright idea one day as I watched people arriving at the dump in their pickups and trucks. First they drove onto the weighbridge and the weight was noted. On the way out, the vehicles were weighed again and the driver charged for the difference. What if, I suggested, DSW didn't *charge*, but rather *paid* people to bring their large rubbish to the rubbish dump? How many poor and unemployed people would collect whatever they could find and earn a small living, at the same time cleaning up the highways and byways? Sadly no one else thought this was a good idea at all.

We made several programmes for the City Health Department on selling food, and how to clean up afterwards. Several of Durban's informal markets are situated under the massive flyover which carries the N3. This is the main highway connecting the city to Pietermaritzburg, ultimately leading to Johannesburg and Pretoria, situated in the area known as the *Reef,* over 500 kilometres away.

This is the most insalubrious area of the city, noisy, dirty and crammed with the minibus taxis which are a law unto themselves. On our outdoor location, we worked alongside the '*muti*' sellers, whose wares were spread out on groundsheets, containing all kinds of potions and powders to make *you* well, or *your enemies* ill. Among the piles of dried leaves nestled monkey skulls, tails from various dead animals and bones of all sizes. To me these represented the darker side of the work carried out by the traditional healers who were beginning to buy their herbs and plants from the municipal nursery. I would watch fascinated as it was not only the local *sangomas, inyangas* or witchdoctors, but the ordinary people as well, who stopped to haggle, bargain and discuss what would best suit their needs to combat spells or cure diseases that many in the west believe are, as yet, incurable.

I was taken aback on a shoot for the Health Department when we went to use the house belonging to one of their clinic nurses as a location. I can't remember the story now, but we needed to show a home situation after the owner had suffered an accident.

We piled a borrowed wheelchair into the back of the crew van and collected our 'patient' and drove into the local township. From the outside the house looked neat and tidy and our nurse welcomed us in with true Zulu hospitality. We set-up in the kitchen and while Shezi was plugging in the lights, I glanced around and couldn't believe my eyes. This was the home of one of the top clinic nurses and it was absolutely filthy. The walls were thick with grease, the sink full of dirty water, there were piles of unwashed dishes, pots and pans everywhere and the utensils on the shelves looked as if they had never travelled to the sink at all. The floor wasn't much better, and I hastily declined her kind offer of a cup of tea, even though I knew that it was highly impolite to refuse.

Like many of the programmes we made, this one also factored in the necessity of keeping everything clean and germ free, besides our constantly carping on about hand washing, an old favourite. I found it hard to understand that while this nurse was trained to teach all these things to the patients, she did not practice them herself. Not only that, she had known for over a week we were due to shoot there, and yet did not see the dirt where she prepared her own food. People are always full of surprises.

There were many different council departments and we made programmes for all of them. We covered road safety and I learned how to fill up potholes. I don't think this has been particularly useful in my life, but I guess it's good to know how things are done.

We also made a video to plead the case for the Museums Department who were facing a severe lack of funding. We were to show the function and importance of telling the story of Durban's past. This was a real treat for me, as history is my second love.

Durban has a house, fully furnished exactly as it was in the early settler days. It's tucked away on a small side street, and beautifully maintained. But few people ever went to see it as it was hardly publicised. After the 1994 elections, all thoughts turned to the future and very few for the past, with one exception.

Another building was acquired and turned into a museum telling the story of apartheid, and Brian rescued a lot of early video footage and re-edited several films for visitors to watch. Far more emphasis was put on this museum than on the original large one in the centre of town, where the exhibits traced the story of the first white people to land in Durban bay and the growth of the town itself.

In South Africa there was a frenetic rush to wipe all signs of history pertaining to the white man. Cities and roads were re-named, companies dared not sound too European. Nothing, we are told, happened before the first free and fair elections, except for the ills of apartheid.

I was quite amazed when I moved to Spain to see how they celebrate their past. Many towns re-enact the battles between the Moors and the Christians in memory of the time Spain was under the domination of the Muslims from North Africa.

I love Africa and I love the African people, but why did they not follow the mentorship route and make sure that the indigenous people were well trained before they took over? When I had my own production company I offered to mentor students on many occasions, but only once was this taken up, and then the guy wandered off after the first day, never to be seen again.

A lot has to do with mindsets, and this reminds me of a call I had one day from a young man who was just starting out in the video industry and wondered if we could have a coffee and chat so he could get some tips.

"Fine," I told him, "No problem. I am only too happy to help."

I'm not sure if he really wanted any information or advice, because he began by telling me how well connected he was and how he would have work coming out of his ears very soon. I was genuinely pleased for him and the conversation then wandered on to politics, as it so often does in South Africa. I listened for a while as he told me how great the ANC (African National Congress – ruling party) was and what good it was doing for the country, and how they were going to be in power for the next one hundred years at least.

"But what would happen if say, at the next election the Pan African Congress party got more votes and they were elected to parliament?" I asked him.

"That would never happen!" he exclaimed in horror.

"Well I agree it's highly unlikely," I continued, "but perhaps the ANC had introduced a law they thought was good for the country, but the people didn't agree, so they changed their allegiance and voted for another party."

He didn't even stop to think. "Then we would have to get our guns and fight them and kill all of them of course," he pronounced firmly as if that was the only obvious answer.

I should have known - it was democracy the African way. What made this more alarming was that this young man was well educated, well turned out, and had friends in high places. He had access to more money than I would ever see in a dozen lifetimes, but his mindset was on another plane altogether.

But back to the council and their unceasing efforts to improve lives, while its twelve thousand employees earned money to improve the lives of their own families.

We made programmes about the dangers of electricity, thankfully not too many. Being such a coward I treat all kinds of power, seen and unseen, with the utmost respect.

We also wrote about the different grants available for those most in need, and highlighted the sad fact that there was a fifteen year waiting list for council housing, and we struggled to suggest as many other avenues as we could think of for alternative accommodation. Frankly there weren't any, except building a better squatter house.

We were constantly explaining the difference between storm water drains and drains designed for wastewater. It was a popular practice in the townships to lift manhole covers and hide stolen property in the pipes. The moment it rained, the surrounding houses were often flooded as all the channels were blocked with the illicit contents of other people's houses.

I had written a scene where we showed a *skabenga* (the Zulu word for a criminal) who went to hide a large bundle down a storm water pipe. Unfortunately we had employed an actor who was horrified at what we were asking him to do.

"You want me to winch that large metal plate out of the hole?" he asked in amazement.

"Yes, that's right."

"This one here, over the drain?"

"Yes that's right."

"How?"

This was something I hadn't considered. "I think you might be able to lever it up and then shove it to one side." I hoped I was being helpful.

"With what?" enquired our actor with a fair bit of sarcasm in his voice.

"Um..." I looked around. There was plenty of rubbish lying everywhere, but broken bricks, rusty tin cans, Coke bottles, old paper bags and short bits of half-rotten wood were not going to do the job. Then I had a brainwave. "A tyre lever would be perfect! Carl, we can use the one in your truck."

Carl looked less than impressed. "What if it breaks? I'll be stuck if I have a puncture."

"Well possibly we could claim on expenses for a new one? We could describe it as a 'necessary prop' maybe?"

I took advantage of his nervousness as he watched a

snarling, *frothing at the mouth* township dog sidle closer and closer.

"Let's get this done quickly, and we'll be out of here before you get rabies," I suggested as cheerfully as I could. I was wondering how to surround Carl with water, like a portable moat, as I vaguely remembered that rabid dogs are afraid of water. I looked around but the community tap was on the far side of the dog and I would have to walk round him to get to it. Also, I did not have a container to put any water in. I considered sacrificing Carl's lunchtime bottle of Orange Fanta, but decided against it. We would just have to work quickly and pack up before the dog attacked. Anyway, I was pretty sure they could cure rabies these days.

Meanwhile Carl was nervously eying up the animal and probably thought it wiser to arm himself against the dog, which had now dropped down onto its hindquarters and was snarling and baring its teeth. A tyre lever was better than a camera to ward off an attack anyway, so reluctantly he collected the lever and even more reluctantly handed it over to our actor.

It's amazing how determined these *skabengas* are, it's not easy to remove a manhole cover, they are really big, really solid and really heavy. It must be very hard work being a criminal I thought, as I watched our star heave and strain and perspire as he struggled with the metal cover. In the end Shezi had to help him, so now we had two *skabengas* on the job, but I promised our assistant we would dull the scene down, pretend it was night time, so as not to destroy his reputation with anyone who might watch the programme.

Eventually we got the shot of them creeping away, satisfied they had hidden their stolen goods, but we did stop shooting while they removed the loot from the drain before replacing the cover. We didn't want to have to open it twice. I decided that if there *was* a next time, we would bring someone from the council with the proper tools and we would pretend our 'hero' was opening the cover all by himself.

Since Durban is a coastal town, it was inevitable that we would be called on to film offshore. The first time, we went out in a small boat to shoot the sardine run. This is an annual phenomenon during which a gigantic shoal of millions upon millions of tiny sardines swim north parallel to the coast. It's a time for the local fishermen to cast their nets and make a killing, figuratively and literally. One of the marvels of nature is the swirling formation the fish hold as they swim close to the shore. It looks like an inverted funnel under the water.

I can't remember the reason why we needed underwater shots of them, it was probably for that crowd at the Tourist Board, but we hired an underwater camera and set off early one morning.

Everything was going very well, Carl and the camera disappeared beneath the gentle waves and I relaxed on the boat thinking that I couldn't believe I was being paid to bob around on the warm Indian Ocean on a bright, sunny morning.

A few minutes later he surfaced and we ran the tape back to look at the first few shots. They were good, but maybe a few more just to make sure, from this angle, and that perspective? Carl was about to drop over the side again when one of the men handling the boat made an unfortunate remark.

"Not a lot following them this morning by the look of things."

"Not a lot of what?" we asked.

"You know, the big ones, sharks and the like. They like sardines, the run always attracts the predators."

That was quite enough for Carl. "I'm not going back in," he declared firmly.

"No, don't be ridiculous, just one more dive." I wanted those extra shots.

"Not a chance."

"Come on, you're brave. We want one from right inside the shoal."

"No!"

He did have a point. I was very keen to get more footage, but no amount of cajoling or bullying would get him back into the water and believe me I tried very hard. Carl was just selfish enough not to risk his life for the brilliant pictures I wanted. Of course I couldn't dive in myself as the wet suit was far too large for me, even if we could have swapped clothes in the small, rocking boat. That was one time that I didn't get my own way. I can just imagine the crew in Hollywood refusing to do what their director ordered!

For our next offshore video, we were asked to shoot a demonstration on how to use the new jet skis the municipality had bought for the lifeguards. This time we would not have to get into the water, as the crowd of sun-bronzed, adventurous and active guys bounced over the waves in rubber ducks and the shiny new jet skis. They took me out from the shore in a rubber duck at high speed, flying over the water, while I hung on for dear life, just for the fun of it. I hadn't written that bit into the script, but I wasn't complaining.

We spent a couple of days showing how to refuel and service the jet skis and then it was off for a ride on one of those as well. As usual we didn't have a very big budget, so there was no money to pay a cast to act the rescue scenes. I had counted on using one of the lifeguards, but they were not too keen. They didn't want to pretend to drown and then be fished out of the water, it really wasn't very good for their image, they explained. What if their girlfriends saw them in distress pretending they couldn't swim?

So I went for a stroll along the beach and asked a couple of middle aged holidaymakers if they would help us. Maybe it was the way I described the programme, mumbling the bit about it being a training video for the Council, but the couple jumped to the conclusion they were going to be on national television (as I had hoped), and they were more than happy to help. I could tell they were on holiday from Johannesburg or the Highveld area, as although their accents were South African they were not suntanned. Surprisingly, you don't get a tan easily at 6,000 feet above sea level, but please don't ask me why. I also guessed that she was from the big city, I had lived there once myself, and no one I knew in Durban would be sitting on the beach festooned in gold jewellery, with all the makeup perfectly in place. I was also a little suspicious about her perfect hairdo as well.

The husband jumped to his feet with alacrity as we explained we wanted him to swim a little way out and then pretend to drown. The lifeguards would then come and save him. We would like him to do this a couple of times so we could shoot from different angles. Was that OK? Yes, no problem at all. He was only too thrilled to be in the movies.

Off he ran and splashed about in the water, and on cue he started 'getting into trouble'. Quick as a flash, muscles rippling in the sunlight, the lifeguards sprang into action and jumped on the jet skis. It was possible they'd not assembled one correctly after yesterday's shoot as it refused to start, but eventually they all raced off and performed the pretend rescue. Only it wasn't pretend any more.

It was for real.

Our poor swimmer had *not* been acting out there, waving his arm in distress. He was in dire straits, made all the worse by the time taken for one jet ski rider to help the other start his machine. We think our swimmer may have had a minor stroke. By the time they brought him back to shore, his poor wife was quite distraught, as they dropped him back onto his beach towel. He lay there unmoving until finally they realised he was in trouble. The lifeguards began the usual resuscitation routine and his wife was weeping and wailing loudly, her gold jewellery jangling as she waved her arms about and wrung her hands. She even failed to notice that her blonde wig was now hanging over one ear.

It's at times like this you have to be professional, and I viciously urged Carl to keep rolling, right up until the ambulance, sirens blaring and lights flashing, had disappeared out of sight down the road.

We did of course check later at the hospital, and our victim was discharged with no lasting harm but, if I wanted realism, I got it that morning and the programme was a great success. I would like to add here that we were not so callous in the edit as to show any visuals of the frantic wife with her make-up running and her wig hanging askew, and our victim had pretty much recovered before they loaded him into the ambulance.

There was one shoot we could only start late in the evening, as the subject was the new Municipal crèche that had just been opened with great ceremony by the mayor (sadly no free nibbles this time).

Usually, new programmes, first time announcements, competitions, the unveiling of innovations, launches of new publications, and... well just about anything you could think of, was a good excuse for a party with free nibbles and drinks thrown in. It gave us all a chance to dress up and beat a path to the City Hall for a few hours of relaxation. There were times when the Video Unit was called in to record the event for posterity and then it was a working evening for us, but still great fun.

This one was a very low key ceremony. The limousine roared up, the bodyguards jumped out and the Mayor crawled out. He mounted the couple of steps to the front door, mumbled a few words to the effect it was good to have a place where night workers could leave their children at five o'clock in the evening, and then pick them up again in the morning to take them to school. In the meantime, they could work their late shifts in the hotels and restaurants and 24 hour petrol stations, knowing their children were safe and well and getting a good night's sleep.

Then he quickly cut the ribbon stretched across the front door, before jumping back into the mayoral limo and they all roared off again.

I thought it was a brilliant idea too, and the plan was to interview a few of the mothers at work, for example behind the reception desks in the hotels, or in the kitchens, or the all-hours fast food joints.

I was seriously naive. We couldn't find any mothers who were using the new facilities. We went back to the crèche and enquired where we could find the working mums, and the staff provided us with a list of their work addresses.

Off we set again, but when we arrived at the first place, we were a bit taken aback to find it was a brothel. Slowly we walked inside, to see a row of smartly dressed ladies, knitting, swapping recipes and touching up their makeup. Were their children in the all-night crèche? Yes, wasn't it a great idea?

I don't know why I should have been amazed at these pleasant, chatty ladies, discussing what to put in their children's lunch boxes the next day, as a different species just because they had a different job. I had never knowingly met a prostitute before and yet again I realised how compartmentalised our lives are. Most of us move in a very narrow circle of friends and places and occupations, and we seldom cross the line into another, parallel world.

We tried the second address on the list and yes, it was

also a brothel where ladies of the night were waiting for custom. Even though Carl was well known for his love of cute babes, by now he was getting hot under the collar. He was terrified that someone would see him going in and out of places like this, with me of all people, and he didn't want word to get back to his new girlfriend.

We could hardly shoot right inside the brothel either, so we called it a night, and went back for further instructions. The programme was never made, and I don't think the crèche stayed open very long either. Urban legend has it that the mayor nearly had a seizure when he realised what he had done and remembered all the press photos, but it was too late to do anything about it.

The next department to ask for a programme was the Durban City Police Force who wanted a recruiting and instructional video, showing all the exciting things a policeman gets to do, while not forgetting to mention how well the city ran the first municipal police force in South Africa.

Now this was going to be fun as they were happy for it to be as long as an hour, so it called for a full script of the proportions suitable for a television special. Once again I wrote a simple scenario of the trio of young lads meeting up a couple of years out of school, and our hero is telling the others what fun he was having working for the City Police. Needless to say the other two had very boring, everyday jobs, where they were never called on to chase criminals, speed down the freeways at high speed with lights flashing, sirens going and adrenaline pumping, nor learn to shoot guns and so on. Very, very briefly, we rushed past the more mundane parts of the job such as helping doddery old ladies across the road, the mindless patrols, and the traffic duty where you learned to tap dance at the intersections at peak rush hour if you didn't want to get your feet crushed.

One of the highlights was our trip in a speedboat through the harbour, as we filmed a chase along the quayside from the water, and another was the traffic accident at night, when we mocked up a young girl being hit by a car while crossing the road. It was all carefully choreographed and shot in slow motion at first and then speeded up in edit. With careful cutaways, even I shuddered when I saw the final scene. Apparently we spoiled it all when our hero policeman bent down over the victim to check for a pulse. He put his fingers on the wrong side of her neck. The only excuse I can come up with is that not one of the crew or cast had been trained in First Aid. But, after seeing the traffic accident, the car chase, running after criminals, leaping over walls, interaction with slobbering and grateful citizens, it looked so exciting even I was tempted to sign up!

Just as I was feeling really confident I could write and direct a programme about anything, I got a shock. I travelled a few kilometres up the highway to Durban North an area that, before the suburbs combined into the Uni-City, had its own mayor and council. It was all very upmarket, and they had great plans for the future, and wanted a marketing video to help persuade businesses to locate north of the city. It sounded very exciting as they showed us huge pictures of the hospital, the amazing shopping Mecca at Gateway, the new housing developments and the stunning office parks built around landscaped lawns with fountains and statues in strategic places.

I couldn't wait to get started, and decided to do a recce first to look at all these amazing constructions. They handed me a lay-out of the roads showing where everything was and as soon as the meeting was over, I walked back out to the car and drove off to see for myself.

I couldn't find them.

They weren't there.

They didn't exist.

The hospital was a shell, work on the office parks had not started, except for one building in the middle of a field, and the shopping mall was a few concrete walls in a huge sea of mud.

It dawned on me that we'd not been shown photographs of these places, but artists' impressions. On radio of course, you could pretend that everything was in place, but for television and video, that was not going to work.

I despaired. How could we go and shoot muddy fields and hope to attract new businesses and residents to the area? It looked less than inviting, the way it was now, no one would want to move there.

The idea came that night, when I woke up in the middle of a particularly nasty dream. That was it! We'll set it in the future and call it '*I Have a Dream*', (with apologies to Martin Luther King).

And it worked!

We showed a brief shot of the construction men hard at it on various sites (building I mean), and then slowly dissolved the picture into the artists' impressions. You could do a lot more today with graphics, but in the mid 1990s things were not nearly as sophisticated.

The evening launch of the campaign was great fun. There were lots of compliments on the movie and of course plenty more free nibbles and drinks. Lots of important people were invited: politicians, community leaders and King Goodwill Zwelothini kaBhekuzulu himself honoured us all with his presence. He took time out to take Shezi aside and heaped praises on him for making such a wonderful video.

I saw Shezi bask in this unexpected glory, thrilled to have been singled out for a personal conversation with the King. I wondered if he might introduce us and mention that we had helped a little with the production but no, there was not going to be any recognition for us. In fact, as King Goodwill walked past us he briefly eyed the camera equipment, mixing desk and other paraphernalia we had brought to record the evening, but he didn't seem to notice us at all.

I don't think there was a municipal department that did not request videos. Besides the ones I've mentioned there was also the Fire Department, Durban Transport, Health and Safety, Treasury, Training, Procurement, City Hall, Election representatives, and Tourism. Everyone made full use of the Communications Department and the video unit, which made each day at work different and exciting. I felt I was so lucky to leap out of bed on a Monday morning, looking forward to going to work. But there were darker moments as well... sometimes I realised just how big the gulf could be between the old world and the new and how little I really understood.

Lots of people go to live and work overseas, but often do not get to know other cultures on an intimate level. I had no idea what it was like for someone with little or no education to understand the first world urban economy, or even many everyday scenarios. There was so much I took for granted and I found easy to deal with. For example, I was really puzzled when I watched my domestic worker attempt to mop up a large puddle of tea she spilled on the kitchen table. I saw it spreading out towards the edge, but she plonked the cloth firmly down in the middle, swirling it round and round, sending the liquid flying over the edge and on to the floor. It didn't seem to occur to her that she was making the spill worse, and now the floor would need cleaning as well.

I watched another middle aged domestic worker failing to piece together a child's nine-piece jigsaw puzzle, which reminded me of the time I was halfway through one large puzzle when the maid tidied it all away back into the box! I guess it's the lack of practice of special skills when very young? There is so much we take for granted, so much we imitate as small toddlers that shapes our behaviour and our understanding. There were times when I wondered if this gulf could ever be crossed in a dozen generations.

I had a big wakeup call in my early days in Durban when I met an amazing lady called Elizabeth while filming in a squatter camp just outside the city centre. She was one of the revered ladies in the area, who had built herself a substantial house from bricks and opened her own spaza shop (the name in South Africa for a small tuck shop) in a simple lean-to next to it. Here she sold Coca-Cola, biscuits, cleaning products, crisps, soap and tinned goods.

She had paid for her two eldest children to go to university and, after obtaining their degrees, they both had good jobs and were, in turn funding education for the younger children. It was the first time I'd been invited into a shack, and I was amazed to see carpets on the floor, a television, a gas cooker and a leather lounge suite.

I begged her to let me write her story for one of the magazines, but she refused. She did not want to draw attention to herself, but suggested I wrote about a young couple who had recently moved into the settlement. I could feature them instead and write about the problems they faced.

A few days later, I met Elizabeth on the road just outside the camp, and she took and introduced me to Joel and Thombi. They were a really delightful couple and spoke quite good English. I was invited to sit on an old Coca-Cola crate outside their packing case shack. In no time, Thombi had the water boiling and handed me a cup of tea African style, that is, laced with spoonfuls and spoonfuls of sugar, and I sat back to listen to their story.

I learned that they'd come to the city to find work. Thombi did not have an identity book which, by law, all South African citizens must carry. Without it she could not get a job and couldn't afford to travel back to her home to ask her mother for the papers to allow her to get one. At 24 years old she was very much in love with Joel, but they did not have the money to get married. When they met, Joel had been working in a butcher's shop, but he had been made redundant, so they were forced to leave their small house and move to one of the townships while Joel looked for casual building work.

Then they heard about the squatter camp where they would not have to pay any rent at all, so they used some of the little money they had left to move there. It took Joel four months to build their house, partly from bricks buried in the ground left behind when the original houses in the area had been bulldozed after the Indian residents had been evicted. He mixed mud and bought some packing case wood for the frame. They got a cheap tarpaulin for the roof, but it wasn't a structure that would stand up well to high winds or a heavy downpour. There were no windows, but they managed to buy a cheap door.

Joel's pride and joy was his radio, but he had not been able to listen to that for months, not since the batteries ran out.

Thombi's most treasured possession was her photograph album, and she showed me pictures of her on the farm where she grew up. She looked healthy and plump, but there was no future there, no chance of work, she told me.

They owned very little and I took photographs of the inside of their house, where Thombi had papered the walls with pages from old magazines and those free supermarket flyers that are dropped through letter boxes. Above her bed I could see advertisements for cut-price margarine and cornflakes on special offer.

Both small beds were up on bricks, as protection against the *Tokoloshe* (the evil water sprite which could attack you while you slept), made from simple wood planks, each covered with a thin grey blanket. There was no money to pay for mattresses.

Each morning Thombi walked to the pump to collect 25

litres of water which cost a few cents, but she had to shop at the more expensive tuck shop close by as she had no money to travel into Durban to buy food. On good days they ate twice, but often there was only one meal and they frequently went hungry. Thombi cooked on a fire just outside the front door and, as far as I could see, her kitchenware consisted of two plates, a jug, one iron pot, a kettle, four enamelled tin mugs and an assortment of knives, forks and spoons.

Yet their few clothes were carefully hung up on a hook and Joel proudly showed me the brushes he used to polish his shoes. Both were very house proud, but it was hard keeping the house dust-free in the camp, with its dirt paths and rubbish piles scattered everywhere.

Thombi also told me that Joel suffered from TB, and although he was attending the clinic it was often difficult for him to work for many days at a time. She proudly added that in the meantime they did not sleep together as she realised that she might get the disease as well. They could not afford children, so that was another dream for the future.

I later discovered they were eligible for benefits from the welfare department, but it had never occurred to either of them to ask for any type of help. Despite their poverty, they were cheerful and optimistic that things would get better for them in the future. They were so upbeat, so hopeful and enthusiastic, and I felt so very humble. In comparison I had so much, and I still wanted more.

The couple asked me to visit whenever I liked as they were only too happy to talk. They were proud of what they had already achieved, building their own house and just about coping in the city. I offered them the few rand I had in my pocket, but I didn't have much to give them. If you were wise, you never walked around with lots of cash, muggings were so frequent. It was dangerous enough carrying your cell phone. But that was something you never left home without and even today it's with me all the time.

When the article was published in *'Personality'*, a national women's magazine, it caused quite a stir. Letters flooded in from Pretoria, Johannesburg, Cape Town and many places in-between. Most of them asked how they could help, lots of letters had cheques enclosed.

The editor phoned and asked me to do a follow-up story. They were putting together at least two pickup trucks worth of goods, candles, clothes, blankets and even some small pieces of furniture. Would I go back into the squatter camp to take photographs and write another story on the day all the goods were delivered?

I was so thrilled, I'd wanted to raise awareness of how some South Africans lived and it had obviously touched many hearts. I had highlighted the optimism and the hope these young people had and how they had cheerfully planned for the future, with all the faith in the world that things would get better for them.

The following week I met up with a couple of magazine staff and one of their readers, and we arrived at the simple shack and unloaded all the goods. When Joel and Thombi saw what we'd brought they were ecstatic, and quite a crowd gathered around to watch. I took more photographs and gave Thombi copies of the ones I had taken on my first visit.

When I drove home a few hours later, I felt like Mother Theresa. I had done some good, I had improved lives, and how wonderful that was! This was the reason I had become a writer, it was destined that I could make a small difference. All the hard work and struggle had been worth it.

It must have been six months later when I was back filming in the same squatter camp, and I kept a look out for Joel and Thombi but I couldn't see them anywhere. However Elizabeth, my spaza shop lady, tracked us down. I smiled as I saw her approaching, but she didn't smile back, in fact she looked angry, very angry.

"I hope you are happy now," she spat at me.

"What! Why? What have I done?"

"You've ruined Joel and Thombi's lives, that's what you've done."

"But, how...? What's happened?" My heart sank.

"You brought in all that stuff, and it caused a riot. Everyone came to take the goods away from them as soon as you'd gone. Joel got into a fight and now he is late." (She meant that he was dead.) "Then they beat Thombi and chased her away."

I just stood there. I didn't know what to say. Elizabeth had one parting shot for me.

"And you got money for writing about them, didn't you? They got nothing."

From feeling like Mother Theresa, smug and self-satisfied, I now felt like Judas Iscariot. Had I profited from a sweet, innocent couple and sold them for a few rand? I cried myself to sleep that night. While I may have had the best intentions, I was still ignorant of customs in another culture.

The next day in the office I went to talk to Themba who also worked in Communications, told him what had happened, and asked if he could help me understand it all. He explained that jealousy is very close to the surface among many Africans, and some who are not succeeding, or are too lazy to do anything for themselves, would either steal from, or even attack, those who had made it.

I remembered my talks with Reggie, my black cameraman when I worked in Johannesburg. The only way he could see to get ahead was to leave South Africa. I also remembered talking to married teachers in one of the Pretoria townships who explained they had erected a three metre wall around their house topped with barbed wire, and drove in and out of their gates as quickly as possible. Their neighbours were so aggressive, so jealous and angry they couldn't afford all the nice things the teachers had, and they frequently threatened them.

So it seemed that even if you wanted to get on, and you attended school, and worked very hard, it was not a passport to an easy life for many Africans.

From that day on, I have been very wary of donations by foreign companies to hand out to the masses. We need to understand if, in the long term, the donations improve, or destroy the recipients' lives.

4   MEETING MANDELA

As a kind of penance I asked the magazine if I could do a piece on the white beggars who were beginning to appear in the centre of town. Again the perception was that in South Africa all whites were filthy rich and all blacks were overworked, downtrodden and poor. This was not a fair picture as, having lived in several other African countries, it was only in South Africa I saw middle class black people for the first time. In other places it had been the government people and their affiliates in the lap of luxury, and everyone else in dire poverty.

I set out to look for some white beggars. I had noticed two or three in the main streets outside one of the large upmarket clothing stores.

I approached one gentleman and told him I was writing a piece for the magazine as I wanted people to know that white people too could become victims of poverty. He was happy to talk to me, but refused to have his photograph taken as he did not want his family to recognise him.

He was the first of many I spoke to and I heard some very sad stories over the next couple of weeks. In many instances, it was a case of '*There, but for the grace of God, go I.*' I was still hanging in there by the skin of my teeth, trying to re-build my life from scratch and claw my way out of debt, but I had not touched rock bottom yet.

For many of the homeless people I interviewed, it was a combination of bad luck, sometimes too much drink, a broken marriage, death of a child, or theft by a business partner. Some fell apart when their partners couldn't cope with a financial or physical disaster and walked away, often taking the children. There were all kinds of reasons why these people had ended up on the streets.

I was sitting on the pavement sharing a piece of cardboard outside Woolworths, listening to one lady who had originally trained as a beautician until her partner had beaten her up so badly she couldn't work, when I felt someone grab my hand. I looked up to see a motherly, middle-aged lady bending forward. She smiled, squeezed my fingers and said "I hope things will soon be better for you. Bless you my dear, I will pray for you." Then she pushed a ten rand note into my hand and briskly walked away.

I was totally taken aback and my first instinct was to jump up, rush after her, return the money and explain what I was doing. I was respectable, I wasn't begging, I was only here to interview, and so on. But that seemed rather crass, so I passed the money along to the lady who was sadly relating her life story as we sat together leaning back against the shop window.

Again, many readers had a heart of gold, and one offer came in to the magazine, to pay for new dentures for one of the homeless ladies who'd had her false teeth stolen while she was asleep on a park bench. I searched the streets for weeks hoping to find her, but she'd disappeared and I never saw her again.

I may have been struggling at that time to support

myself and my daughter, but these experiences made me count my blessings. Being face to face with so many who were struggling day to day simply to survive was a sharp lesson.

I was commissioned to write an article on the high cost of medicine in South Africa. It had come to light that while pills and potions were subsidised for the Army and the State hospitals, this money was clawed back through inflated prices on drugs in the high street chemists. It was a scary story to write as I had no medical insurance at the time and no way of paying for doctor's fees, much less hospital bills.

As luck would have it, a few weeks later I was rushed to the main state hospital in Durban doubled up in pain. At the time, payments were the last thing on my mind, but as soon as I began to feel better, I started hyper-ventilating over the expected bill.

"Not to worry," said the friend who had driven me in. "I told them you were an unemployed writer and, as you are not very good at it, I knew your income was way below the threshold." Looking down he grabbed the chart at the end of the bed. "Let's see, total owing to date, one rand and forty cents, less than a pint of beer!" I didn't know whether to laugh, cry, or feel horribly insulted!

Another article I wrote got me into trouble. I can't remember now who suggested it, but there were several dams around Durban where you can go out for the day, take a picnic, sail or motor on the water and even camp overnight. I was happy to write about them in the 'Metro' magazine (the monthly publication put out by the City

Council Communications Department) to suggest an alternative weekend venue apart from the beach. I had previously written about a day out at the airport and, to be quite honest, in the old airport there was very little to do or see, and I had to spin it out to meet the required length. We called it the *'smoke and mirrors'* syndrome! The client wanted a story or a script, and there was little or no information to write about, so you had to spin something out of nothing.

First thing on a Monday morning, I was picked up by a guy from the Parks Department and in a whirlwind tour we visited all four dams while I scribbled notes about what they had to offer, how to get there and all the fun things you could do when you arrived. What was more, I was thrilled to write that entrance to all the dams was free, so what better way could you enjoy a cheap day out with all the family?

However, the moment my article was published, the complaints began to flood in, by phone and through the mail. The readers pointed out how irresponsible it was to suggest families visited these places as they were not safe. People had been hijacked and one mother wrote that her son had been attacked and was badly injured by a group of thugs who frequented such leisure sites.

On the other hand, there were people who said what a good idea it was and they were planning weekend jaunts to the dams. I just hoped and prayed that no one else would get hurt. I'd often gone to the dams at weekends, but you only had to be in the wrong place at the wrong time to fall victim to a violent crime.

So there was another of life's lessons to learn. If you are

a writer, you can't please all of the people all of the time and, while you might beam with pride as you see your name on an article, or whizzing up in the credits on a television or cinema screen, then expect the good with the bad. If you put your head up above the parapet then you should not be surprised if someone takes a shot at you.

It took a helicopter flight a few days later to cheer me up. I'd been in a variety of planes, but this was the first time I was going to leave the ground vertically. I was really looking forward to it, but there was one thing they'd not told me. I guessed this when I noticed the smirk on Carl's face as we drove to the heliport.

"What's so funny?" I asked him.

"Oh nothing," he smirked a bit more. "You do like flying, right?"

"Yes, I love it, and even that terrible trip to the Drakensberg mountains has not put me off," I replied gaily.

"We'll see," he replied cryptically and put his foot down on the accelerator. I should have guessed, by the happy smile on his face and the way he was humming along to the music, that there was something important he was not telling me. In retrospect, he knew it was pay-back time for not letting him shoot all those cute babes.

While large production companies hire professional helicopters with a glass bubble in the belly, we only had access to an ordinary, everyday sort of helicopter. By this I mean a roundish metal ball-shaped machine, with doors and windows, skids on the bottom and a rotor blade thing on the top.

I just love flying and I was having great difficulty keeping my enthusiasm under control and doing my best to maintain my dignity. Mentally I was already levitating before I even climbed aboard, but when you are approaching middle-age (OK, well into middle-age then) you are expected to behave with a certain level of decorum.

We chatted to the pilot for a few moments, a guy called Johnny, who reminded me of one of those swashbuckling pirates from the movies, full of confidence, full of bravado and a real man's man.

Then it was time to go, and I cheerfully climbed into the back and peered over the front seat to look at all the dials. Carl climbed in beside me and put on his seat belt. I looked for mine too, but before I could push the little metal clip into place, Carl had grabbed it from me to thread through the handle of the camera.

I was about to protest, but then realised if he had to lean out of the window a little way, he would have to stop the camera from hurtling to the ground. There was plenty for me to hang on to anyway I reasoned. Well no, there wasn't. There was the seat in front, but unlike a car, there were no brackets or hooks near the roof. In fact there was nothing to grab onto at all.

The pilot hopped in and started up the engines and we sort of shuddered on the ground for a couple of moments before rising into the air.

I grabbed Carl's sleeve. "Tell the pilot to stop!" I shrieked. "Tell Johnny he'll have to go down again!"

"Why?" Carl screamed back.

"Look," I pointed briefly before grabbing the front seat

with both hands. "Look, he's forgotten to close the door! It's dangerous! We can't fly with the door open!"

"He can't close the door," Carl shrieked back over the roar of the rotor blades and the whistling of the wind.

"What do you mean he can't close the door? We can't fly with the door open! We might fall out! Tell Johnny to go down so we can close the door! We could fall out!" I repeated determined to get the point across.

"He can't close the door," Carl shouted back as I nervously watched the ground recede further and further away.

"Why not?"

"The door's not there."

"Don't be ridiculous, how can it not be there? Has it fallen off?" By now the sweat was running down my face and my sweaty hands slithered around trying to clutch the back of the seat in front of me.

"No, they've taken it off."

"Taken the door off! Why?"

"So I can lean out and shoot!" Carl turned away and began filming but not before I saw that look on his face. He was enjoying this. For once he was in control, while I'm not sure I was even in control of all my bodily functions. I was terrified. This was real payback for Carl and all my moaning about him filming the cute babes for every programme.

I tried once again. "Does the pilot know? Did he agree?" I wanted to make quite sure that he wouldn't be attempting any dangerous aerial manoeuvres. They didn't loop the loop in helicopters did they? Or swoop up and down at dangerous angles and dive bomb and stuff like that?

Not only was I worried about myself, I was also nervous for Carl as I was very fond of him, but at least he had a seat belt on. How strong were seat belts anyway? Would it hold? Would it snap when we were miles up in the clouds? Had they ever been tested holding a person upside down in a helicopter? Probably not, I mean what idiots go racing up into the skies without the doors on? However, I didn't have a seatbelt on at all! If I felt in danger of sliding over towards the open doorway, I'd have to fend for myself and grab anything in sight to stay inside!

There was only the seat in front of me and as my palms got covered in sweat. They slid from side to side. My knuckles were white and my fingers began to cramp. I took deep breaths as I'd read somewhere this was a good thing to do if you had a panic attack. I had a sneaky feeling it also involved using a brown paper bag, but I couldn't see one anywhere.

Carl stopped shooting, pulled the camera back inside and turned to look at me. I could see from the big, beaming smile on his face that he was enjoying every moment of this.

My mind was racing and I shivered with fear. Yes, I was passionate about my work, but I was not really prepared to make the ultimate sacrifice for any programme!

I clutched the front seat even tighter as I took more deep breaths while trying to decide if it was better to have my eyes open or closed. I opened them a fraction and was amazed to see the scenes below. The ships coming in and out of the harbour, the dinky taxis weaving dangerously in and out of the traffic, even the children jumping into the back garden swimming pools.

Usually in aircraft, you go so high so quickly, you don't have the chance to see the details on the ground for long. We had booked two hours flying from one end of Durban to the other.

Once I realised that although Johnny was happy to fly just about tree top height to allow Carl to get the best shots, he was a competent pilot, I began to relax a little and enjoy the ride.

After that, we booked Johnny the cowboy whenever we had to shoot aerials. Despite his swashbuckling manner he was a brilliant pilot, flying just over the roof tops, skirting tall masts and just missing the electric pylons, and with him we always got the best shots. He understood exactly what we needed to shoot and was careful not to bank too steeply. Once I got used to the missing door, I always enjoyed flying with him.

But on one occasion we had a different guy who flew so high we had trouble seeing the city at all! Even the largest buildings looked like dots on the ground, and I think we must have had his cousin flying the day we wanted a full circle shot of the Zulu warrior we had dropped on a mountain top. He had instructions to hold his spear and shield to the sky and invoke his ancestors, while we flew just over his head. Unfortunately the pilot was scared witless, and the results were a small speck waving in the distance. It was not the shot I wanted for a tourist video.

It had taken us ages while we waited for our warrior to kit himself out in his tribal skins, fly him up to the top of the mountain, drop him off then fly in again to film him. We tried to enlarge the shots in edit, but that didn't work, he pixelated and looked quite grotesque. The whole exercise was a total waste of time.

Apart from making educational, instructional and promotional videos, the Municipal Video Unit was also the official recorder of events for the council archives. So when Queen Elizabeth visited Durban in 1995, we were the official team from the city to follow her around. I'd done some research and the last time she'd been in Durban, she travelled with her parents and was still a young princess aged 21.

I was amused when I received a copy of her itinerary given to us by the British consulate, to see that as she left the City Hall, she would make an '*impromptu, and unexpected detour*', to shake hands with a few of the people in the crowd.

For a couple of days we dashed around after her, beginning at the airport where she arrived on a British Airways plane (naturally) flying both the Union Jack and The Royal Standard from the cockpit window.

Now this has puzzled me for years. How do they get those flags out there? I can only think that the pilot must pop these out just before he lands the plane, no maybe the co-pilot that would be safer. I never realised that they could open the windows on the front. Or do they have special buttons to press which shoots a little pole up with the flags already attached? I've had a couple of sleepless nights over that question.

After Her Majesty left the airport it was one

engagement after another. The School for the Blind, a rural school, a trip to the racecourse and then back to the Royal Yacht Britannia which had sailed into Durban harbour so Her Majesty could live on board and play hostess to the Who's Who of South Africa.

Unfortunately we did not have access to go onboard, despite our official badges, but it was a novelty to mix with the crews from CNN, Reuters, CBC and a host of other international television channels. For a few days we felt very important.

We also covered Prince Charles' and Princess Anne's visits to Durban, but I mentioned them in the earlier book.

By this time Durban was the proud home of a massive exhibition centre, always referred to as the ICC (International Convention Centre) built to play host to major conferences. There was the Commonwealth Conference, the Big Dams Conference, the Uni City Launch, the International Non-Aligned Conference, the Undertakers' Conference and the Small Business Conference of South Africa, to name but a few. There was a different event each week, and although we didn't film all of them, we were soon familiar with the venue and enjoyed many a banquet at the back of the hall. I think what impressed me most about the architecture, (and perhaps it's quite common in many other large buildings) was the tiered seating in the largest hall, which could be raised up into the ceiling leaving open floor space suitable for exhibitions.

Since Durban was the host city for all these conferences, and as their official council representatives, we were at the forefront when it came to interviews.

It was at the Small Business Conference in 1997 that we got to talk to government ministers and question several captains of industry on camera, though we were not really expecting to get an interview with the celebrity who opened the conference. But we were in luck, it was on that day that Nelson Mandela gave only one interview. And he gave it to us.

While CNN, BBC, CBC, Reuters and all the others muttered and groaned and moaned, my cameraman and I were escorted through the security and into the meeting room. I could hear loud complaints from behind.

"Who the hell are those two?"

"What gets them in when we've flown all the way from the States?"

"What news channel are they from?"

"They staying at our hotel?"

It was one of the times in my life when I felt positively smug. Meeting the great man however soon wiped the smile off my face. He was absolutely terrifying. He towered over me. I had not realised he was so tall, and he was in a very bad mood. There was a rule that photographers were not to use flash while taking pictures of Mandela, due to the problems he had with his eyes, but that day there had been plenty of flashes indoors as people took shot after shot after shot.

Madiba, (the popular name for Mandela in South Africa) was probably obliged to talk to us on camera as we represented the city which was playing host, but he didn't have to slobber over us and worry about his public relations persona, so he was abrupt, to the point, and did not give us as much as a smile.

I took a deep breath as I asked him my first question about supporting small business enterprises in South Africa. I hoped my voice would not sound too wobbly, the rest of me was quivering, especially inside.

I actually felt quite afraid of him, thinking this was one man I would never, ever like to cross. When the African cameraman and I walked out a few minutes later we were both shaking.

Nelson Mandela had that air of absolute power I'd not encountered before. As a world icon, just being next to him made me feel small and insignificant, and while I'd met several powerful leaders by then, this man was the most awe-inspiring of all of them.

We didn't have much time to sit and talk about our experience, as for the entire week of the conference we were shooting during the day and then editing at night so that, by the end of the week, we would have a video to give to each of the delegates to take home. The official programme for the conference not only covered the events in the main hall, but also some of the smaller meetings taking place in the side rooms. They also wanted a record of some of the social gatherings held in the evenings, so after the first four days we were all totally exhausted. It wouldn't have been so difficult if there had been a lot of people working on this, but I seem to remember there were only about six of us putting this all together.

On the Friday morning, as the delegates arrived for the last time, we had produced a couple of hundred copies of the week's event ready to hand out.

The huge conference of the Non-Aligned nations was hysterically funny. We had a big, raised platform set up at the side of the main hall which was next to the main control desk for the big screens. All the international crews crowded into the hall for the fantastic opening ceremony, followed by Nelson Mandela's opening speech – we didn't get to interview him this time.

The hall was packed, rows upon rows of tables, with the delegates sitting behind their country's flags, most of which we didn't recognise at all. It was a truly impressive sight, and the opening ceremony with songs and dances was really spectacular.

My only claim to fame during this conference is that I fell over Graça Machel's legs. At the time she was married to Nelson Mandela and we had heard she had little love for either the press, or the former rulers under colonial power. I was sneaking round the back of the main seating area and crossing one of the aisles when I stumbled. Why the great lady was sitting on the floor I have no idea, but she glared up at me as I trampled over her knees, and she hissed at me loudly. As quietly as I could, there were speeches going on in the hall, I tried to apologise, but she turned away in the other direction.

However, from the opening ceremony, things began to go downhill and although, like many of us, I do not have a very high regard for politicians, I was astounded to see them behaving more like children. These were not even minion politicians. Most of the countries were represented by their Heads of State and a Foreign Minister or similar.

The cell phone companies at the airport had done a roaring trade hiring out handsets and temporary SIM cards and, as soon as the dignitaries filed out and the next session got under way in the great hall, it seemed everyone got a cell phone out and was phoning non-stop. I think many were phoning their aides and bodyguards on the other side of the hall, but the combined phone conversations were drowning out the speakers at the podium.

On one hand it was funny but then, after the plenary session, nearly all the delegates left. You couldn't help feeling sorry for the next speaker who was talking to a near-empty hall. We were a little bemused. Hundreds and hundreds of important people had flown in from all over the world, at great expense, to listen to words of wisdom, to network and compare ideas, but where were they all?

We were not quite sure what to do as our brief was to record the speakers and we would of course cut away now and again to show the audience listening with rapt attention. But there wasn't an audience. The best we could do was to focus the camera close up on the few bored, security guards posted by the doors and hope they would be mistaken for some senior government minister from a far-flung country.

So, where were the delegates?

They were roaming all over the city shopping, and shopping and shopping. Only a few of them began drifting back to the ICC around supper time, festooned with huge numbers of carrier bags. In desperation, the catering crew came round to find people to eat all the food that was laid out on the tables and was now going to waste. Would we like to help ourselves? This was more than the usual nibbles at functions, and we ate until we burst. It was quite soul-destroying to see so much food going to waste, especially as some of the papers the speakers had delivered that day were bemoaning poverty and starvation.

For the next four days, we sat in a near-empty hall as one lone speaker after another talked to himself on the podium, and then even the speakers themselves evaporated. One night we sat there until half past ten waiting to shoot the early evening session, but no one came, so eventually we packed up too and went home.

Like a reawakening, everyone suddenly materialised for the closing session which was another song and dance routine, a final speech and lots of goodbyes and "See you again in Kuala Lumpur in five years," as they all made for the airport.

Not all the conferences were like that, many had excellent speakers and packed halls, but these were generally centred on engineering, service provision and environmental issues. It appeared that it was the politicians and heads of state who saw no real reason to listen to any ideas other than their own.

There is always the exception, and the Commonwealth Heads of Government Meeting (CHOGM) in 1999, when Her Majesty paid a second visit to Durban, was well attended and everyone behaved very nicely. It was noted as being the largest and best attended CHOGM ever held.

However, the delegates did not behave quite so well during the big international conference on AIDS. Prostitutes, from all over the county flocked to Durban to provide solace and comfort to the attendees, who were far from home comforts and missing their wives and girlfriends. We heard the ladies of the night did a roaring trade, which defies belief since everyone must have been very aware of the dangers of HIV. Surely the visitors were attending the conference to *talk* about how to control and eradicate AIDS, not on how to *catch* the virus!

Each year the Horse Racing Club in Durban has an event similar to Ascot when, for three days, hospitality tents are put up all around the racecourse. There are fashion parades, and thousands of visitors come to eat, drink and have a flutter on the horses. The highlight is the Durban July Gold Cup and, almost since the movie camera was invented, the stewards have commissioned a record of all the important events.

This was great fun to shoot, but hard work. In the earlier days when it was sponsored by Rothmans, we were lucky enough to get free handouts, and we scooped up packet after packet of cigarettes and stuffed them in our pockets. Once it became illegal to advertise tobacco, it was then sponsored by a cell phone company, and they weren't handing out free phones or free air time!

The beauty of working in video for all these kinds of functions is that you were able to visit the celebrity boxes, slide into the weighing room, walk freely around the presentation ring and wave the cameras around the commentary box. You could gain access to most places, proudly announcing your priority status with the badge on the string around your neck.

For every similar shoot for conferences and events you had a security tag and, after the event, we would hang these up in the office in large bunches. They came in a range of colours, shapes and sizes and, if you kept them long enough, you could clearly see the aging process from your fading photograph safely welded inside the sealed plastic cover.

One interesting fact I did learn from a steward at the race course as we walked past a large bundle under a blanket lying to one side is that, on every race day, there was at least one fatal heart attack or stroke. I'm not sure if this applies to every large gathering such as rock concerts, or other huge celebrations, but I found that a very sobering thought.

Maybe this is a good place to briefly describe a video script. I had a template with four columns on the paper. In the first one I wrote the number starting at one in the first box and then two and so on down the page. In the second column I wrote down the visual shot I wanted, for example it might be an opening shot of a sunrise or an establishing shot of the Durban City Hall for example. It all depended on what sort of programme it was. Column four was for the audio or the spoken words, which I would time out and fill in column three with the length of shot we needed.

From the approved script, I would then break it down into scenes listing the order we were going to shoot. You don't film a programme from beginning to end, but rather in small chunks, usually based on geographical location, as you don't want to be running backwards and forwards across town just to shoot in the right order. You might have to do this though, and race from one place to another if you have limited time or budget for a very expensive or famous presenter. You will obviously do all his or her shots in the shortest time to keep costs down. You can't have a famous someone kicking their heels while you potter about getting cutaways, or interviewing members of the public. All that can be done when the personality is safely out of sight and not costing you money.

Continuity is very important whether you are making a

short video or a Hollywood blockbuster. Our programmes were often projected onto a massive cinema-sized screen, and several smaller ones in a large venue, so mistakes were noticed. So while we were out on a shoot, the Production Assistant, (me) along with the Director (me) and Props (me) and Producer (me) and the Tea Girl (me) and the Navigator (also me) logged down each shot on a separate sheet, along with the time code from the tape and a description of the shot number. You seldom get what you want on the first take, and we always took a shot twice if we could as backup, in case there was a flaw on the tape.

Back at the studio, we would compare the shots and choose the best one and then on yet another list, log the time code for the one we would use. There was space for the time code numbers at the start of the shot and again for the numbers at the end. This can take a lot of patience, as we might have taken five or six shots from different angles which could all cover the same words on the voice-over.

Most programmes, say fifteen or 20 minutes long, could take three or four days to shoot, but in the finished version, our story might take place over one day. If we were using actors, I always had to remind people to wear the same clothes, even if it meant running the washing machine, or scrubbing shirts and blouses in the bath every night. In high end productions they have several sets of the same outfits for this reason. At our level of production, I would have to beg people to please remember to put on the same blouse, skirt or trousers if we were shooting over more than one day.

The one time I got into serious trouble was with a professional actor from Durban who was easy to work with but, like most of them, he didn't learn his lines, although I'd sent him the script two weeks earlier. However, I only had to read them out to him once, and he could repeat them to camera without a flaw. He was also really good at walking and talking to camera at the same time, something a lot of presenters find difficult. They can do one or the other, but not both together.

If you don't believe me, try reciting a piece of poetry while walking around the room, remembering to look at an imaginary camera and stopping to pick up something off the table, and you will see it is not easy. I wonder if they practice this in drama schools. This sounds such a ridiculously easy thing to do, but it requires concentration in two areas at the same time. You have to find a cameraman who can walk backwards smoothly so the presenter doesn't look like a kangaroo.

To most audiences, the only important person is the Presenter. They are not aware that anyone else is involved in the production, and frankly they couldn't care less. This can be frustrating, especially for the scriptwriter who has put the words together, for which he or she gets little or no credit. Often, the presenter grumbles about not having access to a teleprompter, but it's not practical if you are out and about shooting on the move. Next time you watch the news, put your nose close to the screen and you will see the reader's eyes move very slightly from left to right following the words as they scroll up on the teleprompter.

On location I would often have to read out the words and then the presenter would parrot them back to the camera line by line. When this happened we had to shoot lots of extra cutaway scenes to cover up the pauses while we practiced the next sentence.

Having got all the footage in the can (I presume that phrase came out of Hollywood) it's time to edit. Now all the shots must be put together in the right order with smooth transitions between one scene and the next. If you make movies at home - and there is some really great stuff produced these days in bedrooms, uh no, make that the spare room - here is one tip to avoid a video looking like an *amateur* production. Most edit programmes on the computer have a whole box of tricks to produce scene transitions. These include falling blocks, wipes, slides, melts and dissolves and so on. But if you watch any old Hollywood movie, you will see they use straight cuts all the time. One scene cuts straight to the next one and most times this is how we edited. If you use too many fancy transition effects one after the other, it's like being in a disco at night and it can make your audience feel quite nauseous.

Once everything is on the timeline (all the pictures on the monitor next to each other in the right order) you can type up and add the titles, record the voice and then add this layer to the video, making sure it is synchronised and people are not talking when their mouths are closed. If you are even one frame out it shows and, when you realise there are 25 frames a second in video, you have to be accurate. Another layer goes on with the music and it all kind of ties together in the final mix.

One of my most depressing moments was in a museum in Mpumalanga Province where they had on display the very first edit suite I had worked on. A couple of weeks later I noticed in the toy museum in Gold Reef City in Johannesburg, they had some of the toys I had played with as a child, marked 'historical exhibits'. Now that is enough to convince you that you are old.

So, back to my continuity problem. In one programme our brief was to give an overview of the main functions of the Water Department. I thought we could tell the story from a runner's point of view as he jogs through town, stops at each interest point, and says a few words about it. Running had become very popular and, as this was for some overseas conference, I thought it would have universal appeal. He starts his run in the morning, and the final shots would take place as it was getting dark. I think the title was '*A Day's Run in Durban*', or something similar.

For a week we moved from place to place, shooting our runner as he approached, said his bit to camera and then ran off again into the distance. It was going really well, until the last morning. Our star was pretty fed up by now, he'd been running for four days and it never had been his favourite activity. His temper wasn't improved by the seventeen takes we had to do on the beachfront, because a couple of real idiots kept making obscene comments, and waving bunny ears behind his head. We simply could not get rid of them.

Added to this, the next shot was our runner racing up a steep hill, there are lots of steep hills in Durban, and it was all getting too much. I couldn't even let him walk and then speed it up in edit, even though it was suggested. Running and walking are two quite separate actions.

Our star was dripping with sweat and totally breathless,

so we worked fast. Finally we agreed to take a short break and meet him later to take the last dusk shots, and around six that evening we canned the final scene and it was a wrap. The presenter waved goodbye and went off to catch a plane to Johannesburg while we went back to the studio.

It was only on the Monday morning in edit that I noticed it. Between the Friday morning beach shots and the evening scenes, the presenter had changed his running gear. He had started off in a plain white T-shirt but, at the end of the day, several logos had mysteriously appeared across his chest. I was appalled, but there was nothing we could do. Our star was appearing in a Pretoria theatre over 700 kilometres away, so we had to make the best of a bad job. I only hoped that no one, including the client, would notice. Nobody ever said a word but, every time I saw the master tape sitting on the shelf, I cringed.

If you work in the industry, it can actually spoil your enjoyment of films and television. If you see a phone in a scene, you wonder when it will ring, or you notice when the continuity is out, or ask why one character is wearing a sleeveless cotton top and the other is decked out in an overcoat with ear muffs and gloves. It happens more often than you think! Everyone is aware of several television programmes showing these mistakes, and I bet half of them are noticed by people who work in the film or television industry.

5   LAST DAYS AT THE COUNCIL

Durban Municipality pulled off a coup three years in a row by getting permission from the government to open an in-house radio station over the summer holiday season, which in the southern hemisphere falls over Christmas. Everyone was involved.

I was thrilled to be back on air again and one of my tasks was to read the news. Unfortunately it was at the time when a certain Mrs Bobbitt in America had deprived her husband of his most precious possession and thrown it out of the window. Apparently she was very cross with him at the time. It was really hard to read this out and sound serious, we all wanted to burst out laughing. I suspect it was no laughing matter for Mr Bobbitt who, I understood, was in hospital having it re-attached, but the disk jockeys would insist on discussing his predicament before they put on the next music track and allow me to escape from the studio.

It was a really active station and, besides music, we had quizzes and lots of phone-ins with prizes and interviews with all kinds of people. I was given an assistant and between the two of us, we would line up a selection of local celebrities and citizens and list the questions we wanted to ask them.

One guy owned a game park not too far away, and in return for the free publicity we gave him during the interview, he invited me and the crew to come and stay over free of charge and film the wildlife. We had a magical three days stalking giraffe, hippo, rhino, warthogs and the rare sable antelope.

That little trip wasn't without incident as we had walked out to try and film the hippos at dusk. They had persistently and selfishly stayed under the water during the day, flatly refusing to have their pictures taken, and I hoped we could use the sun gun, (a small light mounted on the camera) to get a better glimpse of them just as they were coming on shore to eat.

Although we wandered around the main lake for some time, there wasn't an animal in sight, so we decided to give up and go back to the rondavel. I had just turned round, and was leading the way back up the grass track, when I heard the unmistakable low grunts of hippo communication very, very close by. I took off like the wind, breaking out into a cold sweat while desperately trying to remember how fast hippos ran. Yes, cheetahs could get up to 80 miles per hour, but hippos? I had a sinking feeling that they could run faster than a man, and certainly much faster than I could go as I stumbled forward, gasping and heaving, until it dawned on me that Carl and Shezi were not with me. I looked back only to see the pair of them bent double with laughter. As soon as he saw me looking, Shezi let out several more realistic hippo grunts. I could have killed the pair of them.

A couple of years later this same game park was the venue for my own wedding, my second, and also the second ever to be held there. Now it is a well known and popular venue for both weddings and honeymoons.

* * *

A large textile company in Durban donated hundreds of beach towels to give away as prizes on the radio. Even if we'd had a quiz every ten minutes we couldn't possibly have given so many away. Every day they delivered more of them, and the piles grew higher and higher and like furry triffids, they began to take over the studio. When the broadcast licence expired in the January, we still had mountains of towels. It got to the point when the manager was urging us to take a couple home every night.

"We've got nowhere to put them all!" he exclaimed. "They're cluttering up the whole studio, and we're not allowed to give them away in the street or sell them." I still have three in the cupboard, they have lasted very well and still urge me to '*Be Beachwise in Durban*'.

Another spin-off for me was writing the radio adverts along the lines of public service information. There were reminders not to go home without your children, and we exhorted the listeners not to swim naked in the sea, nor use the beach showers to wash their laundry. They should not light fires or sleep on the sand and please use the toilets provided. It was just your general everyday information to make life more pleasant for everyone on holiday by the sea.

In the days when apartheid was alive and well, it became a show of disobedience for large numbers of black Africans to go down to Durban beachfront on New Year's Day and pour onto the beaches. The political parties organising these protests would hire buses and send them to outlying villages and townships to bring the people in. Thousands of people happily hopped on the coaches and by the time they were all settled on the sand it was almost impossible to put a pin between them. They specifically made for the areas that had previously been labelled '*Whites Only*'.

There were some rather rude comments made by the SABC reporters in Johannesburg, about the state of the crowds, proclaiming that millions had descended like locusts. The message was clear. Avoid Durban beachfront like the plague.

Well the Communications Department could not let that go unchallenged, and hired a helicopter and flew in low on New Year's Day and took still photographs of every inch of the sand. These were blown up in super-fast time, laid out on the studio floor, and members of staff knelt down and did a headcount of each and every beach frolicker. Now they had the correct facts, and could send the statistics straight to the SABC in Johannesburg.

This was another first for me as we packaged (just a smart term for knocking together a video) a short three minute insert with the right information, and I was sent along to the SABC in Durban to see that the footage was beamed by satellite to Johannesburg. Now that does not sound the slightest bit amazing these days, but back in the mid-nineties, before everyone had Skype and Face Time, I was fascinated and not a little impressed.

Carl came with me and on the way back out we were accosted by one of the television presenters. She was frantic and asked desperately if either of us could work a camera. Carl lit up like a beacon and beamed happily as he told her that was his precise job.

"I need to record the links for the footage we've just

got, but I don't have a cameraman. Could you help?" she pleaded.

"Sure, no problem, but I don't have a camera, maybe if I..." Carl went to go back inside, but she grabbed his arm.

"The camera is over there." She pointed to a flower bed.

Carl walked over, and sure enough, there was a camera lying among the flowers and just beyond it was the presenter's cameraman, out cold.

"He's been drinking," our new friend said. "We've been down on the beachfront, but when we got back, he passed out."

I looked at the young man, dead to the world, and I wondered what his career plan for the future was.

As always, Carl was delighted to help a maiden in distress. He rescued the gear, recorded her links to camera and she scuttled inside to the edit studio. Ah, the modern changes in South Africa, you saw something new every day.

The following year, although the hierarchy in the news department mentioned there were a lot of people on Durban's beaches, they did not make any disparaging comments, but I can't recall if they ever broadcast our short insert. I have a feeling they didn't.

It had become another tradition for the mayor to visit the beachfront on New Year's Day, and as a good PR exercise, we were asked to go along and film him smiling and shaking hands and welcoming the tourists. I don't remember him kissing any babies though.

We all met up in one of the seafront hotels and were escorted out to a pick-up truck and set off at a slow drive along the promenade. Now I knew that the mayor seldom moved far without his bodyguards, but I didn't expect them to arrive wearing cool dude shades and adorned in bright, floral, fluorescent Hawaiian shirts which bulged suspiciously at the hip and under the armpits. I would have felt more comfortable if we had not been accompanied by armed guards, who were so obviously pretending *not to be* armed guards.

I don't think anyone ever took a potshot at the mayor, but I was very glad when our short 'meet and greet' was over. What we didn't notice at the time was the commotion at the opposite end of the beach. The lifeguards had raced into the water and rescued a man, but as they tried to resuscitate him on the shore, they were surrounded by a mob of drunken louts who prevented their efforts. The poor man died. There were always a few who drowned in the sea, even though the water is shallow and considered a safe bathing area, but so many people could not swim and did not realise the dangers.

After everyone had climbed back on the buses to go home, there were always a couple of dozen children left behind. While some of them were quite distraught, others did not seem to mind at all. They were housed in one of the local schools, fed, watered, entertained and given toys and a comfy bed.

Maybe their parents were simply too inebriated to notice, or simply forgot, or believed they were returning with the same number of offspring they had brought to the beach. Either way, it always took a few weeks to reunite all the families, and I heard that sometimes the parents were none too pleased to see them back again.

Durban has a vibrant economy, but is always keen to

attract more industry, especially from international countries. It was decided that a promotional video was needed for the overseas market, but what was the best way to really make the point?

"I don't want to script this programme," I said.

Everyone looked at me in astonishment I had never been known to turn down any work in the past, what was wrong with me now?

I explained. "I think we should let local businessmen tell it in their own words, that makes it more authentic and the viewers will be hearing the facts from people they can relate to. Could we make up a list of respected business owners and ask them questions to camera with cutaway shots of their businesses and the other things they are talking about? We don't want it to be all be 'talking heads'. This is the phrase used for a programme where you just watch one person talking to the camera all the time. These are so boring as to be useless getting any message across, remember the 'clunk, click' syndrome? The idea is to grab your audience and hold them captive. That's the reason so many programmes, especially American series, show you some of the action before they break away for the titles and the commercial breaks. They hope you will hang on in there to find out what happens, and not go surfing the other million and one channels to find something better.

For the promotional video, it took me a couple of weeks to track down all the business people we wanted to feature, and a couple more to interview them. It then took hours and hours as I watched all the tapes and chose those sentences we needed from each one. Once that was decided, we edited them all together and we were thrilled with the result.

We had highlighted the excellent electricity services, the potable drinking water, the good schools for children, the nice houses, the low cost of living, the easy access for transport and export. We left no stone unturned, and we delivered the programme and sat back and waited for the enthusiastic praise to come flooding back.

It didn't happen.

There was an uproar and the programme was withdrawn, it wasn't going to be shown anywhere. Why? Two of the eminent people we had interviewed had since been indicted for fraud and were under investigation. One was already languishing in jail. Could we please edit them out?

This was a disaster, as we had moved seamlessly from one person to another and back again, so we would either have to replace them with other people, or go back to those people who, so far, were squeaky clean. Many of them were not available and more shooting and editing would require more money. I don't think that programme ever saw the light of day.

What amazed me was that every single one of the people we had interviewed had been so nice and so friendly, it was difficult to think of any of them as criminals.

After the 1994 elections when Nelson Mandela became president, there were local council elections held throughout the country. Now everyone had a vote, they could choose not only the national government but the people to represent them at local government level as well.

Carl and I were sent out to shoot a brief record of the ballot boxes which had been brought back to one of the municipal buildings, ready for the votes to be counted the next day. There they were, rows and rows of them on the floor, but as I moved a couple around to allow Carl to walk between them I noticed that a fair few had the seals broken.

I looked at Carl. "What do we do?" I asked him. "Do we show the broken seals, or pretend they have not been tampered with?"

This was tricky as we had not been given any brief other than to shoot them. We sat and discussed this for several minutes and decided that we would do both. First, we would run several minutes of stock footage of the boxes looking untouched and then, on a separate tape, we would show the real state of the others which had been broken open. The client could choose which ones to use, it wasn't our decision. More propaganda, I thought as we packed away the gear and left the building. It also occurred to me there was no kind of security keeping watch on the boxes, and had we been dishonest, we could have had a field day in there destroying votes, with no one to stop us.

Another urban legend that did the rounds was the refusal of the Inkatha Freedom Party to take part in the first major elections. At the last minute, Chief Mangosuthu Buthelezi relented and millions of new ballot papers had to be printed which now had a box to tick if you wanted to vote for the IFP. It was said that the number of ballot papers which flooded into the townships far exceeded the total population of South Africa, even if you included all those under the age of eighteen who were too young to vote.

However, once the papers were counted, it was time for the new councillors to take their seats, and I'm not sure where the directive came from, but the Communications Department was asked to produce a video explaining what a councillor did, and how he or she should behave. Now that they had been voted in, it was time to tell them what they had let themselves in for.

We held a long brainstorming session and it was quickly decided the cartoon approach was the best way to go. We would have to use cartoon people of course, but we must not make them black, or white, or brown, or even yellow. It was not so much a question of being politically correct, but one of not being prescriptive. It was decided we would have grey people, which seemed to be a good compromise.

This video might have a very long shelf life, so we went right back to the beginning of the process. We began with an explanation of how prospective candidates could register and some ideas on how to persuade people to vote for them – absolutely no intimidation, threats, bribery or violence, none of these were allowed in a true democracy. It would not be acceptable to wave guns in people's faces, nor set fire to their homes, kidnap their children or kneecap them if a member of the public did not seem too keen on voting for them.

Since the elections were over, I hoped it wasn't too late to explain all this. Maybe there were a few people already hobbling around with no knee caps.

The vote counting procedure was explained and then

came the responsibilities for successful candidates. Firstly the need to attend council meetings, and ask the people who had voted for them what changes and improvements they wanted in their community. All this had to be balanced with the party line, which was a bit tricky.

Then there were other things to consider that I'd certainly not thought of. For example, it was not acceptable to instruct municipal workers on how to do their work, they already had clear instructions from their bosses. Nor was it permitted to order council workers to labour on their private houses and gardens. In other words, although they were now on the council, this did not give them a workforce of over 12,000 as their own personal employees. Apparently this came as quite a nasty surprise to many new councillors.

We also included the usual: no bribing, no giving contracts to friends, no threats or cajoling to get other councillors to vote the way you want them to. This was a radical mindset change for many of the prospective candidates when they were invited to tea and nibbles and a viewing of '*How to be a Councillor in the New Democratic South Africa*'.

I was also very surprised to learn that a candidate was not required to know how to read or write, or have any formal education at all. This was to make it fair for all people wanting to be part of local government. But I wondered how they would be able to carry out their duties effectively. What if they had to sign papers? Would they know what they were putting their thumbprint on? Surely it would be very easy to coerce or fool them? I was assured this wouldn't happen but I was not totally convinced. In fact I wasn't even the slightest bit convinced.

About this time I was approached by a production house, which was putting together a radio series about what your vote allowed you to do. As usual I wrote the series in drama form, but I was a bit dismayed when I realised for the first time that there was very little your vote could give you. When I researched and saw what the people had been promised, I was even more dismayed.

Even in the squeakiest-clean democracies, a vote does not give you any money, nor will it provide you with shelter. You can't eat it, wear it or sell it, or even exchange it for something more useful. A vote doesn't seem to be the magic answer to life after all. I was reminded of the quote from Karl Marx:

"The oppressed are allowed once every few years to decide which particular representatives of the oppressing class are to represent and repress them."

Was this to be the culmination of all the years of armed struggle, loss of lives and great personal sacrifice? Was the end result the creation of a new oppressive class, where the few at the top were now ready to offer their version of repression?

I couldn't believe I was thinking this way! I'd always been a staunch believer in democracy, but now I began to wonder if it was the only answer to governing the masses. I shrugged and carried on writing.

I had been instructed to try to lower the expectations of the post-election period. Life would go on as before, with the only slight difference being you just might have the opportunity to approach your elected representative and mention improvements you would like. Whether he would ever follow this up, was a moot point, and I didn't labour that. A vote was simply a one-off chance to catapult into power anyone who could gather enough support. The whole exercise made even me think long and deeply about the rather dubious costs of South Africa's new freedom. The bottom line was that only an elite few would benefit in the short term and possibly even fewer in the long term.

In the following years, I met and interviewed several people who held positions in local government and I got the impression some of them were quite ruthless. I chatted to Jacob Zuma at the Durban Club one evening and I must admit I was not the slightest bit impressed. As he handed me his business card, he was telling me proudly that he had not done too badly after only two years of formal education, although the internet tells me he had none at all. He was Minister of Tourism in the Kwa-Zulu Natal Provincial government when I met him, and held many other important posts in the African National Congress that I wasn't aware of. I was quite shocked when he later became President of the whole country, as I had spoken to many other politicians who seemed much better suited to the role.

I think I must have filmed in every part of Durban and the surrounding areas in those years. We even filmed firemen sliding down poles, wading about in foam and putting out fires for the *'Fireman's Olympics'*, and we worked hard creating a special programme to support Durban's bid to host the 2008 Olympics. We thought our idea, of using local children from all nationalities to present excellent reasons why Durban would be an ideal host city, would impress everyone. The climate was right, a lot of the infrastructure was in place, we offered a sea level venue and a couple of large rivers and mountains nearby could be used for those events which needed rivers and mountains.

Sadly, the bid to the South African contingent was turned down, I believe the National Olympic committee suggested Cape Town instead. In the end, I don't think their bid got very far at all.

I became very sneaky, and if there was somewhere in the city I wanted a better look at, then I did my best to write it into a script. For example when I discovered there was a tunnel running under the harbour entrance, I wangled this into a programme and off we went to shoot there. I began to feel I knew every inch of my adopted town.

Our cameraman was absolutely amazed to discover that under most streets in cities there was little solid ground, but miles of tunnels and pipelines and conduits for water, electric and sanitation purposes.

As we all know, things never stay the same, life is constantly changing. I had enjoyed every day of my work with the Durban City Council, not only in scripting and directing the videos, but also writing speeches for two of the mayors, articles, interviews, attending the conferences, trips to Cape Town and Johannesburg to award ceremonies, and the joy of being back on radio.

Several people left the department, a couple more retired and many of the new projects became very political and dealt with policies and political correctness rather than the educational side, which I felt was more important and relevant.

Since I had continued as a freelance 'employee' I had also written a couple more radio series for the SABC in Johannesburg and worked for other clients in Durban, but work at the municipality was definitely slowing down. I had no idea what was in store, and was beginning to fret that I would not be able to pay the bills and put food on the table, when out of the blue, another door opened.

6   OUT ON MY OWN

The young assistant, who had worked with me on the radio at Christmas, recommended me to the organiser of a new project being implemented by the Kwa-Zulu Natal Provincial government. It was sponsored by one of the five major banks and a large, international accounting group.

The idea behind this project was to encourage the different provincial departments, such as health, transport, education and so on, to improve their service delivery and their customer relations. The aim was to put the people first and work in the best possible way for everyone's benefit and the winning teams would receive an award.

Several of the provincial departments spread throughout the province had entered, firstly by filling in a plethora of forms, and then by hosting a team of eminent judges who came to inspect them. The finalists would be filmed in action, and the culmination would be an invitation to a lavish awards banquet held in the ICC in Durban. There the winning teams would be presented with an impressive trophy either in bronze, silver or gold to display in their work place. Every finalist also received a very impressive certificate signed by the sponsors and the premier.

This was a whole different ball game for me. For the

first time I would have to prepare and type up a full quotation, and I'd never done one on this scale, not when I was responsible for paying all the bills. Before I even started, I needed to cost out the whole exercise. I knew if I got it wrong, I could end up deeply in debt, not only by under-charging but also if I was not able to deliver the completed video on time, and to the standards they expected. In that case I would have to return all the money. Money I wouldn't have, as I'd have spent all of the first payment.

I was absolutely terrified, but needing silly everyday things like food, a roof over my head and internet, you know, the essentials in life, all convinced me that I would have to make it work somehow.

I wrote down all the things I would have to pay for: petrol, salaries, video tape, equipment hire, accommodation, and so on. Every time I looked at the list it grew longer and longer, and then I'd remember even more items. As I added yet another expense I got more and more nervous.

As I had done before, when I went to be interviewed at the very smart Durban offices, I blithely assured them I was more than capable of doing the job. Oh yes, a walk in the park, no problem at all! Yet again I was kidding myself. I'm very good at that.

Now, as I looked at the horrendously high total at the bottom of my list, I gasped. They would never give me this much money would they? Maybe, to those at the top this might be peanuts, but to a lowly freelance scriptwriter and director and ex-teacher. What was I doing?

Reason took over. If I dropped the price and I asked for

too little then I was really in trouble, so sink or swim I would type it all up and brazen it out.

It was early the next morning, before I was due to take the proposal in, when I suddenly realised that I had included everything I could think of in the quote–except money for myself! I'd put in a bit for contingencies, as I had read about those somewhere, but if it went in as is, there would not be a cent extra for me! You can see what level of competence I had in the commercial world, quite sad really. I had budgeted the whole quote which included me working for absolutely nothing!

I got out the calculator, worked out how much the Council had paid me for a day's work and doubled it. I reasoned that as I was now taking on more responsibility and it was a 'do or die' situation, I might as well make it worth my while. The final total was now much larger, but I decided to take the risk.

Much to my amazement they seemed to think my quote was reasonable and then I mentally kicked myself for not asking for a whole lot more. It also flashed into my mind that cheap pricing also indicated you were either trying to do something on the cheap, or you were not capable of doing a job properly as you didn't really know what you were doing in the first place.

They scribbled their signatures on lots of different pieces of paper and the die was cast. I was now responsible for completing an hour-long video, featuring eight different finalists doing eight different things, in eight different places spread out across the province of KwaZulu-Natal. I was about to cover an area over twice the size of Holland, so I would need to factor in the cost of maps as well. We were still languishing in the dark ages, no one had even heard of a GPS unless you were about to set sail into the Indian Ocean.

Since I was new to this project, the facilitator came with us to shoot all the finalists. Most of the different venues we would be able to reach on day trips, with just two or three nights away.

To add to my discomfort, the sponsor's representative then arrived with eight box files, each stuffed full, containing all the questionnaires, the judges' reports, and an extra file which outlined all the aims and objectives of the scheme.

I opened the one on the top of the pile and realised it would take me several weeks to get through just this one and I pushed the lot aside in despair. I had really gone over the edge this time. I felt totally out of my depth, and wasn't at all sure that I would be able to brazen this out. I would just have to use my common sense and bring this down to earth. The target audience on the night of the awards would be local provincial departmental workers of all grades and the idea was to encourage them, not scare them to death. It was quite enough that this director and scriptwriter was scared to death. No, wait, I was a producer now wasn't I? I raced to look it up in the dictionary. Yes, I'd had a promotion, well a self-promotion if you want to split hairs. Who says women can't multi-task? I was now enacting so many different roles I wasn't sure where one began and the other ended.

A couple of weeks later we set out. There were four of us and because of all the equipment we took two cars. I had hired a cameraman I'd worked with before, and a

Metro City policeman who was on leave to do the sound. He'd already appeared in two Hollywood films, '*Ghandi*' and '*The Lion Hunts in Darkness*'. He was happy to be involved as it meant experience of production work, and I was happy to have him as not only was his radar well tuned to any problems, he also came with a gun strapped to his ankle.

I had travelled extensively around Durban, but this time, we would be going out into the deep rural areas and I had no idea what to expect. There were rumours about frequent attacks on the farms and civil unrest, and it was unlikely this would be broadcast on the national news. The new democratic government was not prepared to acknowledge that things might be getting a little dangerous in some places.

As each day passed I began to relax, especially as our guide supplied by the financial company, made it very easy for us and I began to see what the scheme was looking for. We visited a health district in a rural area, which had kept its clinics open day and night, and was also busy training health workers who would visit patients in their own far-flung communities.

One social services department had been checking all their registers, to remove those who had put their names down fraudulently for benefits. They told us that it was quite common to 'rent a child', the more the merrier, to take into the office for the interviews assessing their needs. One sharp-eyed clerk suddenly noticed that she had seen those same children several times that morning on each occasion with a different mother! They took action.

Another finalist was a veterinary laboratory, which

fascinated me as they had a huge locked store apparently housing, among other things, containers filled with live rabies! I couldn't help but walk on the other side of the path, just in case! With their mobile laboratory and information centre (a rather elderly caravan), they were taking information out to the rural farmers and smallholdings. They were also one of the first departments to actually ask their customers what they wanted. This was quite a novel idea in a country where it had always been assumed that those in charge knew best. I stared in fascination as I watched a laboratory technician inject eggs with a syringe. Now that was worthy of an award in its own right, I just knew I would smash every egg if I tried to do that.

We visited a school in a deep rural area which originally had four classrooms with 80 pupils in each instructed by three teachers. This was hard work for them, especially as the cattle grazing in the grounds disrupted the lessons. In only a few years, with the combined help from teachers, parents and the newly formed governing body, they had installed ten toilets, fenced in the grounds, built fourteen classrooms and encouraged the parents to pay fees. With this money they converted three classrooms into a hall, which they charged out to the local community for weddings and other celebrations, and they'd also revamped their vegetable garden.

It was good to see the toilets as on another occasion I met up with some Scandinavians who had offered to build toilets for one rural school they had just visited.

"Oh, no," the headmistress replied. "No, we don't need toilets, the children always use the bush. We need computers, we can't teach the learners anything without computers."

Local businesses had been persuaded to donate equipment such as a photocopier, fax machine, a duplicator and typewriters and fund security guards to keep out undesirable elements. It reminded me of Aggrey Klaaste and his *Nation Building* initiative in Johannesburg. It *was* possible for people to do things for themselves. The staff and parents of this school had not waited for some foreign aid agencies to present them with handouts. They had worked together to provide an excellent learning centre for their children.

The same hospital I had been in just a few years ago was also on the list, and this time I saw it from a completely different point of view. We shot their in-house radio station, an orientation ceremony for new staff members, and the centralised cardio-pulmonary loan unit. I had been quite dismayed when I noticed there was a hospital on the finalist list, I'm not good with 'biology' stuff, and since the council shoots never took us to more than the local clinic, I was reminded of my previous gruesome experiences.

They began when I fainted in primary school after being shown pictures of the nervous system, followed by my eviction from biology lessons in high school. Every time they carved up a piece of dead animal I hit the floor. If I visited a hospital the sight of an intravenous drip was enough to make me pass out completely, and the sight of blood had me quivering like an aspen leaf.

But as long as I averted my eyes and nudged the cameraman to take the shots so that I didn't have to peer too hard at too much blood and gore, I coped. I didn't pass out once which was a point of great personal pride. To be fair, we were not looking for the blood and gore sort of shots, our angle was on the administration side and happy patients.

The other two finalists we filmed were both involved with transport, and did not bring tears to my eyes in quite the same way as the rural school, but they had certainly made improvements to the service they were giving their customers. I was a little taken aback at the team-building games they were all playing during work time. This was the first, but not the last, time I would come across this phenomena and the whole thing made me rather uncomfortable, watching adults horsing around without a drop of wine in sight. I told myself there are some perks to being freelance. If I'd been asked to run round a circle of colleagues and pretend to be a horse, or a cow, I would have just died of embarrassment.

From feeling quite despondent about the high levels of fraud, corruption and other crimes we read about every day in the papers, these were heartening lessons, and while these projects would not make the headlines, they were beacons of hope in the darkness.

I must admit to being in a bit of a fog during that first series. Our subject specialist was very academic and I was not quite sure exactly how she was judging one project against another. I could only see amazing initiatives, but they had been measured by a list of aims and objectives and paperwork and form filling. I tried to look as if I knew what was going on, but to me, the improvements just spoke for themselves.

On the night of the award ceremony, attended by the premier and lots of important people high up in government and business, we set up a four-camera shoot and recorded the evening. The video was shown to a hushed audience, who watched with rapt attention, and it dawned on me that not only was the provincial government recognising good service, it was also passing on ideas and things to copy. In the following weeks the programme would be shown as part of the travelling road show, visiting several towns throughout the province. This would spread the word even further, and I hoped we were helping to make a difference.

While the client had paid the first fifty per cent upfront before we began work, I had spent all this before we had got to the ceremony. It was a bit nerve-wracking as I waited for their final approval and for them to process the remaining amount of money. When it finally landed in the bank, I could hardly believe my eyes at the huge sum, and was about go wild and buy myself a whole bar of chocolate when I paused.

I had no idea when I would get any more work, and I had even less idea how long it would be before I earned another cent. I'd heard enough tales about companies going under due to cash flow problems, which is simply a posh way of saying they had no money they could lay their paws on.

I paid the last outstanding bills and hoarded the rest. To be fair, I had by now re-married, so my position was not as precarious as it had once been, but I was determined to pull my weight and contribute at least fifty per cent as my share of the monthly running costs. These had leapt up alarmingly as we now had a mortgage on a beautiful house north of Durban.

All our children, we had two each, were now in the final stages of tertiary education, and one had already left to go and live in London. None of them could see any future in the new South Africa and over the next few years we would take them one by one to Durban Airport and wave them off on their way to a new life in Europe.

At that time, we were not planning to leave South Africa. We certainly didn't believe in the practice of following our children around the world, they had their own lives to lead. I'd even heard one story where the parents had packed up and moved to Australia to stay near their son, and three months later his company sent him on a five year contract to Alaska.

Things had changed a lot since I first went to live overseas. In those days it had taken weeks for letters to fly back and forth. Now, we had Skype and we often had longer chats with the children now in London, than we'd had when they lived down the road.

But it was no good sitting and wishing we could all be together, and it's not in my nature to sit and do nothing. I had, almost without meaning to, begun a new stage in my career and I hoped that I would get more of the *'People First'* projects.

I started one practice on that first major shoot and kept to in the following years. I'm a total dummy when it comes to maths, but I can add up, and each time I hired in crew or facilities I would offer a set rate for the work. I paid good rates, but the amount was fixed. Sometimes I would get the benefit, for example if we worked over time, and it may surprise you to know that our industry considered ten hours to be a normal work day. We seldom stopped for lunch, but at least I always packed food and drink for the crew, not every producer did. Sometimes the crew or facilities would get the benefit if we finished ahead of schedule, and I always made sure I was totally prepared before I went into the edit suite. At hundreds of rand per hour cost, even on a fixed rate, I had not budgeted for extra days if I went way, way over schedule.

I introduced another new idea. As soon as a job was finished I paid the crew and where possible, most of the facility bills as well. It was common practice in our industry to pay everyone when the producer was paid by the client, but this could be many weeks later, and since we were all freelance, we had to live in the meantime.

I always managed to hire the best people, those whose passion for good work matched my own. In turn, they would choose to be part of our team as they knew they would be paid within 48 hours of presenting their invoice.

I worked with the most talented people, who were a joy to work with and we could have put our own team up for one of those awards. We all pulled together, no one ever moaned about long hours or asked for overtime and, what is perhaps most important, we all felt an enormous pride in our work. We poured our hearts and souls into every programme we made.

While South Africa has been criticised for many things I was brought up short when I paid a visit to Britain later that year. As I stepped off the plane and queued up to go through passport control, there were large notices everywhere warning you not to abuse the staff, either by using bad language or threatening them. Though generally patient, even I was ready to be extremely sarcastic by the time I finally reached passport control. We'd had to wait for such a long time because only two counters were manned, and after an eleven-hour flight, standing in line with swollen ankles was enough to make me very angry.

The penalties, the poster on the wall added, were extremely severe and could lead to enormous fines or even imprisonment. It was really intimidating and this was practically the first thing you saw when you landed on British soil. *'Don't mess with us'* was the message blazoned loud and clear. I thought it was such a nice introduction to Britain and was sure that everyone noticed the warm welcome which would give them a nice fuzzy feeling inside.

When we returned to Johannesburg after our holiday, I did a double take at the posters on display at passport control at Jan Smuts airport. These urged all passengers who did not experience good service from a smiling and welcoming employee to phone a number and make a complaint. The airport wanted their visitors to have the very best service and be happy with the welcome they received on entering South Africa. They hoped all travellers would enjoy their stay in this beautiful country.

What a totally different mindset! It seemed like the wrong notice had been pinned up in the wrong airport. The chances of being mugged, hijacked or gunned down in South Africa were way, way higher, but the people were certainly friendlier. You could guess you would be robbed with a smile and a reminder to 'have a nice day' as you picked yourself up off the pavement. I was glad I was living in a country where they wanted to give good service. Whether this always happened was another matter altogether, as we were about to discover.

While I had been recommended to shoot this first initiative in KwaZulu-Natal, I learned that each of the other eight provinces was preparing to introduce the same scheme. But new regulations had been implemented and everyone would have to tender for any work, and before you could even do that, you had to be on an approved register for service providers.

To qualify for approval, you had to have so many 'points', and only then could you be put on the procurement list. This new regulation had been put in place to provide work opportunities for the 'previously disadvantaged', and encourage them into the workplace

I now had a problem. I could claim a few points for being a female, but that was as far as it went, I got zero points for being white. The only way I could see to survive was to form a company and take on two partners, so that between us we might have sufficient points to get higher ratings.

I immediately knew one person I wanted, an Indian lad who had worked with me to get his practical experience to complete his diploma in video technology. I knew within the first day that he had a natural talent. Making good movies, even small ones like ours, is a skill that can't be taught it's like writing, you either can or you can't. You can learn the tricks, the layout and how to research, but no one can tell you how to think of a story, or an interesting camera angle that somehow gets the point across in an innovative way.

Not only was I happy to team up with him, but we would gets lots of points for a 'previously disadvantaged race'. As a bonus, he was younger than 35, so he also fell into the youth category, more brownie points.

I also chose a friend, a black African lady who worked at the SABC. She would be involved as and when her work allowed but, in the meantime, she was happy to come on board. As an African and a female that gave us major, major extra brownie points.

I registered a company legally and everyone signed masses of papers, and we all trailed from the bank to the accountant's office then on to the tax office and back to the bank, until the ink had finally dried on the last piece of paper.

We were now set to go and tender for more provincial government work. As the scheme was being rolled out in the other provinces, I hoped that this would put food on the table and, if I could get to grips with the official requirements, then I was willing and happy to film more finalists including their award ceremonies.

However, in the unlikely event I was hired to work in all nine provinces, I would not be able to do them all, as many took place at the same time of the year. I also had to find out when they were calling for tenders, if I missed the listing in the Government Gazette, then I stood no chance of being appointed. I still needed to find other clients.

Several of the larger private and corporate companies were having a hard time, and did not have a lot of money to spend on videos, but the South African government seemed to have buckets of cash to spare.

In the meantime, Brian had left the City Communications Department and had set up a small studio, renting a room in a larger production house. Taking a deep breath, plenty of tranquilisers, and a bank loan, between us we bought a broadcast quality camera, a lighting kit and a very expensive tripod. We agreed that we would work together as much as possible in the years ahead. The first provincial project came at just the right time, but neither of us could form a company together as we were both white. Whoever got a contract would hire the other as a service provider and we would also look for work anywhere we could find it.

It was a scary step to take, as it used up all our spare capital and we had committed ourselves to monthly bank repayments. We were quite nervous we might not get our money back. However, I had seen how much it cost to rent equipment from the hire company for the two week's shoot I'd just completed around the province, and I hoped that a few shoots would offset the costs of our perhaps reckless behaviour. There was also the insurance to pay every month, now we were the proud owners of expensive top-end gear and there was also the worry of keeping it safely stored away at night.

Every minute we were away on location the camera came with us, into restaurants, dining rooms, waiting rooms, rest rooms, everywhere. That camera was never out of sight and not even left in a locked car.

We were lucky. Shortly after we set up in business Brian and I stumbled on one of the few enterprises which was not short of cash. It was a weight-loss company with headquarters just outside Durban. They had a huge network of group leaders spread across the length and breadth of the country and they had new ideas and practices they wanted to introduce.

Like many clients they had little idea of just how long it took to make a video, another group of people who thought that you turned up with a box brownie, waved it around for a while and then took the completed programme out of the back and handed it over. It's not that people are ignorant, it is just that they've never even thought about the process, I guess, any more than most of us have stopped to think how a tiny potato seedling leapt into a crisp packet.

Of course the script is only the first stage, and like so many others, this company had left it almost to the last minute to order a video, along with several hundred audio tapes. If I was well prepared it would take two days to shoot, with two days of editing, to produce maybe ten minutes for the final programme, and that was only as far as loading all the shots onto the timeline in the right order, with the right dissolves and cuts between each shot.

We always worked on the basis of a new shot every three seconds, which added up to 20 per minute, two hundred for ten minutes, a little less if there are interviews.

Brian would help to keep costs down by transferring the tape at night and we would edit on his equipment together, but of course, he would be the one to push all the buttons. I would record the voice-over and choose the music from the few sound tapes we had bought.

It took exactly two days to go in and record a few groups as they weighed their clients talked to them and displayed their special low-fat products.

"Can I have a go?" I asked after watching dozens of clients being weighed.

"On the scales?"

"Yes please."

"Sure, no problem." But as I was about to step on the machine the lady stopped me. "You must take that off," she said, pointing to my belt.

"Oh, will that make much difference?" I asked.

"You have no idea how much belt buckles weigh," she replied. I'd learned something new.

I was in my seventh heaven after she told me they would not enrol me as I did not weigh enough, which I guess wasn't too surprising since I spent so much of my time out and about on my feet, climbing in and out of vehicles and helping to carry heavy equipment. Video work is quite demanding and you have to be reasonably fit, especially when you are working against the clock.

As soon as we had the visuals on the timeline, I asked the clients to come in and approve the programme before we began the final mix, as it was easier to tweak, add, or remove anything before we went any further. I have to admit the CEO of the company was incredibly helpful and had everything set up for us for the shoot, but then she wanted a whole load of changes which were not in the script at all, stuff she had thought about afterwards. She was also running ragged getting ready for the launch, and we ended up working from early in the morning until late at night. Eventually on the second day, we realised we would have to work right through the night to meet the deadline.

So there we were in the studio at one o'clock in the

morning, the CEO, her assistant, Brian and myself, trying to get it exactly right for them. I heard several loud rumbling noises and realised it was my stomach telling me that I had not had anything to eat for at least twelve hours, and Brian was also close to starvation. We decided to phone out for pizza. We asked the CEO and her assistant what they would like. There was a long, pregnant silence.

"Uh, no thanks, we've brought our own products, they are free from additives and excessive fat and harmful chemicals and MSG and E4 and..."

"Fine," interrupted Brian, "I'll make that two unhealthy and dangerous pizzas for Lucinda and myself."

That was the only time I have ever done a voice-over at three in the morning and I'll swear it sounds quite different to any of my daytime voice-overs! It had a sort of dreamy quality, but at least Brian managed to edit out the yawns.

After working 29 hours without a break, I drove very slowly and very carefully to the audio duplication facility on the other side of town and left them to make the five hundred copies of the audio tapes which were required. Thankfully the client only needed half a dozen of the video programme. I left for home and bed, setting the alarm to wake me to collect and then deliver the tapes and disks to the client five hours later. And the world thinks that working in the media is glamorous!

I've said before that the local African people were a joy to work with, always unselfconscious and willing to role play at a moment's notice, but there were a few exceptions. One was a large supermarket chain which wanted to explain the new bar-coding system that was beginning to appear on many products. It was also another of those great programmes where my curiosity was satisfied as I was taken round to see the large computers behind the system and how the prices could be punched in to match the numbers on the little black lines marked on the packaging.

All went well, until we needed to show how the scanner worked at the checkout. This was its first outing and everyone gathered around to gawp at the glass panel with its glowing red lights twinkling from below. One of the managers demonstrated how it worked with a box of cornflakes and a tub of margarine, swiping them across the window before the price popped up on the till next to him. Then he asked who would like to be on television. Whenever we were seen filming with professional gear, people automatically assumed it would be on broadcast television.

There was a deathly hush in the supermarket and everyone took a step back from the checkout.

"Come on now," said the manager cheerfully, "who wants to be a TV star?"

Without exception, everyone shook their heads.

"Look, I can't be seen to work at the checkout," the manager bleated, "what's the problem?"

No one was prepared to say, but it looked as if the local girls were scared of the glass panel with its shining red light and its magic ability to 'read' the barcodes on the products.

We hung around for several minutes as the shop staff huddled together and whispered in Zulu. It was only the promise of an extra bonus which finally persuaded one brave soul to try it out.

I asked Shezi who was assisting on the shoot what was worrying the girls, he was Zulu and was eavesdropping on their conversations. Knowing Shezi he was sizing them up, he was always one for the ladies.

"They think the rays might burn them, or make them so they cannot have babies," he explained. "They think it will make them ill."

I felt sorry for the manager who'd received instructions from head office to have the whole superstore up and running with scanners at every checkout till by the end of the month.

Much to the surprise of the anxious audience, nothing terrible happened to our new actress, and today in South Africa they are used in every supermarket across the country. It was yet another eye-opener about the culture and beliefs held by people who rode in taxis, used electricity and watched television, but were scared of new inventions and the harm they could bring.

I remembered those barefoot children running over the stripped electric cables in the squatter camps. The people had been told again and again this was dangerous, but this was one real, true fact they chose not to believe. The scanner they could see, the electrical current they could not.

There was an amusing incident when a crew went into the same supermarket to demonstrate the use of the credit card machine. That was back in the days when they put your card on a machine, placed a double slip of paper over the top and swiped a metal bar over it. Then they handed you the paper slip and you signed it, they kept one copy and gave you the other.

As a joke the production assistant who was acting as the shopper signed the slip of paper 'Mickey Mouse', and the cashier never batted an eyelid. Assuming this was because it was only a 'role-play' transaction for the cameras, the assistant then went back into the shop, purchased some goods and presented herself at another till while the crew were packing away. This time she signed the slip 'Minnie Mouse', and again there was no reaction and the transaction slip was placed in the till drawer together with all the other credit card receipts. She thought it was time to have a word in the manager's ear.

Brian and I were commissioned by a lawyer to make two very sad videos to be shown in court. They featured children whose parents were claiming damages, one against a hospital corporation and the other against a motorist. The filming was a harrowing experience even though we had both seen sad situations before.

The first was about a girl, one of twins who contracted meningitis when she was born. She was finally discharged from hospital after three months, but her development was severely impaired. She was now 20 years old, and the family was struggling to cope. It had taken three years to train her to ask for help to go to the bathroom, and she had to be watched every second of the day. She was deaf, couldn't talk properly, and was likely to injure herself, for example by putting her hand in a pot of boiling water, as she didn't have the reasoning to comprehend it would hurt her.

This was one of the most loving families I ever met. Not once in 20 years had the parents shared a night's sleep together. One of them needed to sit up in case the daughter went wandering off in the early hours. The mother was forced to give up her job as a researcher and there was only a part-time nurse, although every member of the family, including the girl's twin brother, did all they could to help.

Even taking her out to the local mall or a restaurant was a harrowing experience for everyone, as they were never sure how she would react. She might begin to wail, or try and take her clothes off, or go to make inappropriate advances towards total strangers. It was a really difficult life for everyone.

They were living in an incredibly small house in one of the Indian townships and all they were asking for was enough money to build on a couple of extra rooms, install some specialised equipment, and pay for 24 hour nursing care.

We spent a week with the family, as they showed us how they coped, and we interviewed doctors and health specialists who all agreed that the daughter was best off in the family home environment. Up until then, the hospital corporation had only offered to pay for her full-time care in an institution, and no one wanted that. The selflessness of the whole family was very moving. It was enough to make you cry and we waited nervously to hear the outcome of the court case.

I think our video must have helped as they were awarded far more than they asked for, and the huge medical conglomerate, responsible for her lack of care at birth, would probably have written the whole episode off as a tax deduction anyway.

The second case was also heartbreaking and both the cameraman and I had problems holding back the tears as we watched this five year old, whose spinal cord had been severed in a car accident, struggle to pull himself up a flight of stairs.

He had been injured a couple of years earlier when his parents, from Atlanta, Georgia, were on holiday in South Africa. They'd returned to the United States and received excellent care for their son there, but it was necessary for both mother and child to be in Durban while the lawyer prepared the case, and then of course for the court appearance itself.

This had split the family. The father had a high-powered medical job in America, and this left the mother to cope with the severely disabled child plus her younger son who was now toddling around and she was pregnant again. Another example of how some people have to cope with the most appalling difficulties and yet give all their time and energy to make life better for their children. As we packed the crew car at the end of the day, we were all counting our blessings.

Again, possibly due to our efforts the courts ordered the claimants what they asked for. I think it would have been impossible to ignore the sad images we had captured and not been moved to tears.

On the lighter side, I was asked to write a script for Patricia Glyn, a familiar figure to many South Africans who know her from her years as a presenter on SABC radio. Two years earlier, while on holiday in England, she had been given a copy of her great, great, grand uncle's diary, tucked it into her suitcase, and only much later, found the time to read it. The day she picked it up she read it from cover to cover.

It told of Sir Richard George Glyn's journey from Durban to Victoria Falls in 1863, and Patricia began to wonder if she could replicate the journey herself 142 years later. Could a woman, brought up in the modern age, cope with the difficulties and hardships endured by her ancestors?

She made the decision to try, although there were differences of course. Firstly it was not practical for her to travel by oxcart, with a few dozen Zulu bearers, and she was not going to linger while she shot game and chased elephants! But maybe she could walk, with backup transport, along the exact route. She would follow the path described in the nineteenth century diary, and keep a diary of her own. She would also write a daily blog, something her ancestor certainly hadn't done!

Patricia's backup team filmed parts of her journey, and it was these clips we were given to put together. My job was to match the short pieces to camera, along with descriptions of the earlier journey and her walk in 2005. I was also given a manuscript of her book 'Footing with Sir Richard's Ghost'.

It was fascinating to compare her journey with the one taken almost 150 years earlier. In some ways it was easier, Durban no longer languished on a mosquito infested swamp, and in some places along the way there were proper roads to follow. But surprisingly her journey traversing the wide open and deserted expanses through Botswana was similar in many places to her ancestor's trek. Once or twice, as Patricia cut across open country, faithfully following her great uncle's exact same route, into areas where her back up team were not able to take the vehicles. Sometimes she was left to wait for them hoping they all had the right co-ordinates.

I never saw the completed movie, as it was sent back to Johannesburg and, as so often happens, we heard no more after the cheque arrived in the post.

Since the area around Durban Bay had been a malarial swamp, no one lived there before the white settlers decided the indentations in the coast would make an excellent harbour. Along with all the other improvements, the new arrivals eradicated the mosquito population, and although the insects re-appeared, none of them carried malaria. I was fascinated on the day we went to one of the university departments, (and I can't remember now why we needed shots of mosquitoes), to see how they were breeding colonies of them.

"Do they still drink blood?" I enquired. Every summer I was often a mass of bites, which itched and nearly drove me mad.

"Oh yes," they told me. "They have a little drink a couple of times a day."

"But how...?" I was really intrigued.

"Do you want to see how it's done?"

"Yes please!"

To my amazement the laboratory assistant left the room and returned with a cute little guinea pig. She showed us how they had given it a punk haircut shave on its tummy, before placing it over a white bucket covered with thin netting. Inside the bucket the mosquitoes went wild and raced up for lunch while the small rodent had its own meal, contentedly munching away at a cocktail of fresh vegetables.

I was assured that none of the little furry creatures suffered in any way from their weekly reverse blood transfusion and they were vital in helping sustain the mosquitoes used in their research. This was just another amazing thing to see and experience.

7 TEACHING & TRAVELLING

When I was approached to lecture part-time at the Durban College of Technology I was quite astounded. I'd trained as a primary school teacher, and you never forget how to teach, but this was something quite different. Towering menacingly over cute little six and seven year olds was a whole lot easier than squinting up at massive great hulks who glared down at me. I wasn't sure I was up to it, in fact I *knew* I couldn't do it. I was scared witless at the thought. Also, how was I supposed to *teach* scriptwriting? Surely you could either write or you couldn't? But the heads of department were rather insistent, so I can only guess they must have been very desperate.

"We want someone who is out there in the business and earning a living from it. You will have lots of advice and practical stuff you can teach them. And you did say you had been trained as a teacher?"

"Well yes, but little kids, you know, up to the age of eight or ten. Some of these students tower over me like the Empire State building! Do you really think I'll be up to it?" I was repeating all the fears I had been thinking about.

"We have every confidence in you," they replied, which was a hell of a lot more than I had!

I was given two sessions a year, blocks of eight to twelve weeks each with the first-year students. The day

I turned up for my first lecture I was quaking inside. No small hexagon tables with cute little smiling faces gazing up at me, and blank walls just waiting to be covered in bright visual aids showing the letters and how to count.

No, this was a vast lecture theatre, with rows and rows of tiered seats housing 79 adults ranging in age from 18 to 49. My place was in the front, with a whiteboard behind me and, on my right, an overhead projector I hadn't the faintest idea how to use. On my left there was a tower of video equipment and a TV monitor, with hundreds of cables trailing from the back of it. I had no idea how to operate that either.

I thought I would open my first lecture by showing them an old '*Impact*' programme we had once made after all the sales people had left and we were desperate for material. This was a television show I had worked on in Johannesburg. It ran weekly and showcased all the new inventions that were about to hit the market and other inserts of general and educational value. This is how it was described in the '*Television Times*', but in reality, it was a thinly disguised marketing programme for major companies since they kept the tapes after broadcast to use as training videos and for display at trade fairs, conventions and so on.

The tape I was clutching close to my chest, to stop the aspen leaf quivering syndrome, showed the procedure of making a programme from beginning to end and I thought it would set the scene nicely. The only problem now, I had no idea how to connect everything up. I had arrived early and looked in vain for the technician they had assured me would do all the technical stuff and would always be easily accessible.

He was nowhere to be seen.

I looked around the deserted lecture theatre and then approached the machinery. It reminded me of something from one of those space movies, wires and cables sprouting from all angles. Maybe I could figure this out? Maybe not.

It's horrendous how pathetic and how often women are shielded from anything to do with machines. Go near anything mechanical and you can hear the screams from China. Anything with knobs, buttons or a cable is not to be touched by the fairer sex, apart from the cooker and the microwave, we are allowed free rein with those. Even picking up the TV remote can lead to World War III.

However now was not the time to be squeamish. Swiftly I crawled behind the tower and examined my options. There were five plugs, but sadly only holes for two of them in the wall behind me. Several of the cables had thin, round, silver connectors, there were a couple that were rectangular and a funny looking white cable with two orange strips running through it. I was stumped. Knowing my luck, if I tried to connect anything I would probably blow us all into the street outside, or next door into the newly opened McDonald's. It was too early for a cheeseburger.

To my horror, several students started to wander in, chattering gaily until they saw their new lecturer crawling about on the floor. They stopped and stared in amazement. There was no other way out but to send one of them to find the technician and in the meantime I would take an inordinate time checking off the register, stringing it out until he arrived.

Ah, I thought of more delaying tactics. I would ask them why they were taking this course, and what they hoped to gain from it. I could make it last even longer if I asked them what writing experience they had to date. With a class of 79, I could string this out for ages, a couple of weeks or more if I spoke slowly and asked them lots of peripheral questions.

It seemed that they had all been extremely good at English, achieved the top marks in their class, and there was more than a suggestion that this course of lectures was probably a huge waste of time. They wanted to be out there in the streets with the camera doing what film-makers did. They obviously didn't think that sitting in a lecture hall was going to advance their careers one little bit. As I was thinking desperately how to reply to all this, the door opened and another student walked in, followed by two more, followed, much to my relief, by the technician who began to work his magic with the spaghetti junction of wires, plugs and cables.

Punctuality gave me another excuse to rabbit on about how important it was to be on time, set up and prepared to roll the cameras well before any event. I must have sounded so pompous, but I was still extremely nervous as I peered up at the tiers of an almost silent and not very eager audience.

At last the tape was ready to roll, once I had dimmed the lights. I turned them all off at my first attempt, plunging us all into pitch-black darkness causing wild whoops and a lot of scuffling before I connected with the dimmer switch. By now they must realise that I was really technically challenged if I couldn't even turn a light switch on and off successfully.

I had forgotten there were a couple of shots of me in the programme as the scriptwriter, at least fifteen years younger with a Jimmy Hendrix hairstyle (I'd had an accident with a home perm), and that caused wolf whistles and shrieks of laughter too. I was not doing very well. At the end of the video I asked if there were any questions, and was met with a barrage of political rhetoric from several of the black African men sitting together wearing ANC T-shirts. This I was not prepared for and I could feel my control slipping away, I was quite terrified. I took a deep breath.

"I am not here today to debate politics, good or bad, in South Africa but I can tell you one thing. You will be asked in your careers, *if* you pass at the end of your third year..." I paused for effect to let that fact sink in, "to provide stories on a wide range of topics. When you write these, you will be expected to tell both sides of the story to give as fair and balanced a view as you can. The viewers are not interested in *your* views, but those of the people you interview or report on. You are simply part of the backroom crew and nobody cares a damn about you. When your names floats up the screen, your audience will already be in the loo, or getting a beer from the fridge, or putting the cat out. If you wish to stand on a soapbox and get noticed, or you want fame and fortune and people to recognize you in the street, leave now and walk over to the drama department."

At this point, to my horror, one student stood up, noisily gathered her belongings together and walked out. I have no idea where she went and don't remember if she ever returned.

I then told them the story of my writing for the potato crisp company on Monday, highlighting the advantages and delights of eating large quantities of potatoes swimming in oil. Then, for the Heart Foundation on the Friday of the same week, I contradicted myself and wrote how appallingly bad potatoes were for you, if you wanted to follow a healthy eating plan and avoid heart attacks.

As an aside, I mentioned my ignorance over the *'acupuncture in animals'* fiasco with the result the programme was never made. This was when I was working for the SABC in Johannesburg, and simply refused to include interviews with people who said that acupuncture did not work and was a complete waste of time. I was not prepared to present both sides of the argument, and only realised years later that I would not have presented a balanced argument.

I reminded them again that the scriptwriter was at the bottom of the heap and many writers never became involved in the production at all, nor invited to the wrap party, or the launch.

They quietened down and I was feeling pretty pleased with myself but, at that moment, all hell erupted outside. I sauntered as casually as I could over to the window to look outside, only to see hundreds of students rioting, attacking the staff cars and throwing bricks, bottles and anything else they could find at the building. One large piece of rubble bounced off the bars outside our window just as the police arrived armed to the teeth. A pitched battle began on the other side of the wall.

No one had told me what to do in a situation like this, but I thought it wisest to stay inside, and told everyone to remain where they were. Of course no one did, everyone rushed over to the one small window at the side and peered out. I hoped it wouldn't further inflame the protesters outside.

To my relief, the head of department came in and suggested that we all took shelter in the largest studio and wait it out while the police got everything under control. I was worried firstly about my youngest daughter, who was a student on the other campus up the road, and secondly about my car. Were they throwing bricks at it? In the event, we all escaped unscathed.

From that first week things went a lot more smoothly and I enjoyed my lecturing. I was always happy to answer questions about what it was like to work in the industry in the real, outside world, but the one question I refused to answer was "How much do you earn?" How could I be sure that one of them didn't have relatives in the tax department?

There are nine provinces in South Africa, and in the following few years we would be shooting in six of them. As the roll-out of the 'People First' campaign worked its way across the country, I was next approached by the government office in Mpumalanga Province.

It was a big step forward for me as an independent producer to attend the briefing, present my tender and give a presentation pitch. It meant paying for my own flight from Durban to Nelspruit, hiring a car at my own expense, and meeting the client and 'selling' my expertise and that of my team. It was quite daunting.

It all went off fairly well I thought, until I got lost

trying to find my way back to the airport outside Nelspruit, which was simply a large landing strip stuck out in the middle of nowhere. I think the only flights they had all day were the one I came in on, and the one I went back out on.

Planning this location shoot took on a whole new aspect. I would need to hire a vehicle for three weeks, plan a route between the ten different locations, book crew and check equipment, reserve accommodation, and make sure I had enough money to pay for every contingency. Yes, to an extent, I had already done this for my first project, but I'd had a lot of help from the company representative and she had booked accommodation for us and been our guide at every venue. This time it was totally up to me. Also, we would not be able to get back home from any of the locations at night, so we would be away for three solid weeks.

There was also a deadline as they had already given me the date of the award ceremony, and there was not a lot of spare time. Like so many others who were quite unaware of what was involved, they thought you pointed the camera and that was it, the programme miraculously appeared ready to show.

Not only did they request a video programme running to five minutes on each finalist, they wanted a booklet as well! I was now expected to write a thousand or so words on each department we shot, and take the still photographs to give to the printer.

Then, they mentioned the biographies they wanted included in the booklet for each of the numerous judges, and a small piece about the artist who designed the gold, silver and bronze trophies (and pictures of those too) and a recap of the 'principles' to go in the front of the book. And then they threw in their request for a piece on the sponsors as well.

I tried not to panic and I wasn't too sure if I'd not bitten off a lot more than I could chew. At the speed of light I added on the cost of the booklet and research and upped the price.

This time I would not have my subject specialist with me, but she was still involved and kindly helped me load my car with ten box files of reports, questionnaires and guidelines for me to plough through before I could begin to write the script.

I stayed up late each night reading and scribbling, until it dawned on me how difficult it would be to film from a script when I had not done a recce. There wasn't enough time or budget for me to travel the 700 odd kilometres to visit each of these places, so to some extent I would be shooting in the dark. I would have to research as I went along and post-script to the video footage we managed to record.

I was also sweating buckets, praying that the deposit would be paid on time. Government departments the world over are notoriously slow at paying suppliers and I would barely have enough money to fund all the expenses. It had still not landed in the bank when the three of us jumped into the car and set off north.

I had planned everything down to the last detail on paper, but I had no idea how it would work out. All I knew for certain was I had the best team Russell and Aarnav my young Indian partner. We all had the same passion for producing the very best that we could.

It took almost a full day to get to Nelspruit, the capital of Mpumalanga Province, and there was just time to settle into our bed and breakfast before the meeting over supper with the representative of the scheme who would clarify matters and advise us of any problems. I had hoped that he'd be coming with us to the locations, but no, he was off on holiday, a relaxing safari in Kruger Park. However he assured us we should be able to find most places and he did have contact numbers for the people in charge at each location. Perhaps we could arrange to meet one of their staff at a known place and they could act as guides?

It all sounded rather casual, but now we were here, we had little choice. I had planned to start with the Housing Department as their offices were in Nelspruit and easy to find. At least it meant two nights in the same guest house.

When we arrived the following morning I left the crew outside to take exterior establishing shots of the building, while I went in to introduce myself. I had to wait my turn as the receptionist at the desk was busy selling hand knitted woollen booties to several interested customers. While I waited, I peeped into the suggestions and complaints box to see it was full of toffee papers. This was *not* an auspicious start.

When I finally got to meet the staff they were not expecting me and were totally at sea. They had no idea what to show me. I reminded them about the principles they had been following *so* well, they had been nominated for the Premier's Award. They were aware of service standards, best value, openness and transparency and so on?

Yes, and they had a Happy Letter to prove it.

A Happy Letter?

Yes, they had come up with the idea of sending a letter to all their clients as each phase on their future homes was completed.

Great! Anything else?

They could show us their plans for the different styles of houses they built.

Brilliant, we can shoot those as well.

And our offices are bright and airy?

I had to explain that I couldn't fill five minutes with a shot of one letter, a few house plans and three rooms with desks and chairs in them. I needed to see some houses too.

They looked crestfallen and warned me that the construction site was miles away and all the department personnel only worked in the office, they never went out there, in fact many of them had never seen the houses they were responsible for planning and erecting.

"Now's your chance," I smiled brightly. "We are doing this for the premier after all!"

After a lightning recording of the interiors and a couple of quick interviews to camera we were on our way out to see the houses, but as we approached, I almost wished I hadn't asked. There were rows and rows and rows of small grey breeze block boxes, with tin roofs and one water tap and one long drop toilet for every four houses. They may have been built close to a main road, but I could see no sign of public transport, and no town or village close by either, so where were these people going to work, attend school or buy food?

I decided to concentrate on the positives, but I was dismayed to see that although we had seen many different and interesting designs on paper in the office, all these houses were exactly the same. Despite the beautiful and varied drawings, I learned that only one design was ever used.

When we got back to our lodgings that night we fell into the routine we were to follow for every project over the next eight years, and it was an exhausting one. We would rise early for breakfast, pack the gear into the car and drive off to be at the first location by eight am, sometimes earlier. We would then shoot, interview, photograph, and travel to any required place to record their achievements and hopefully be through by about four or five in the evening.

Piling back into the car we would then set off for the next location, which might be a couple of hundred kilometres away, and on the way in the car, I would look at the footage we had shot, and then scribble notes for the reports for the booklet.

At the next accommodation we would unpack, have a meal and then I would log all that day's shots and write the audio for the video. I then chose the shots I wanted to use, and logged them separately on a fresh log sheet. Then I would parcel up the film from the stills camera (for the booklet) and get that ready to post to my husband the next day. Hopefully, by the time I got home, the prints would all be ready for me. Should we be lucky enough to be in one place for a couple of days, then I could use a printing and developing service nearby, but this was not always possible.

The only thing left now, was to write the thousand words for the booklet, and if I was feeling creative, I could get that done by midnight. If the words didn't come instantly then I would still have to plough on, 'writer's block' wasn't an option. Those thousand words had to be written, come hell or high water.

Time then to fall into bed totally exhausted, hoping I would have a decent night's sleep in a strange bed.

Each day followed the same pattern, day after day for three weeks, leaving the weekends to catch up on anything that had fallen behind, although sometimes we would shoot on a Saturday as well.

On the long drive home I would play the tracks from a pile of CDs I had packed into the crew car and choose the music we would use under the voice-over. I planned it so we would be ready to start dumping the footage onto the computer the moment we arrived back in Durban. Since I had written the time codes down, once these were copied into the studio computer, only the shots I was actually going to use would be transferred onto the edit machines and onto the timeline.

Our routine was exhausting but it was also exhilarating. We met so many people, saw so much, and received, in most cases, unlimited hospitality. I guess we were lucky, as the majority of the contestants desperately wanted to win the coveted trophy and went out of their way to accommodate us. We were fed and watered, slobbered over, and often the staff would insist on carrying the camera gear as well.

I did try to persuade them that we were not in fact the judges, they had already paid their visits and we were simply here to record their findings, but no one ever believed us. They were determined to impress us to the best of their ability.

That first shoot in Mpumalanga was the toughest as it was the first one on our own, and the Housing Department wasn't too impressive, but our visit to a rural school was another matter. Run by an elderly European, he had forged links with a local chief, so we all trooped off to meet him.

We sat under the baking African sun as we waited for the chief to arrive, as was the custom. In Africa, you wait for important people and the more important they are, the longer you must wait.

Eventually he arrived, resplendent in his animal furs which girded his loins, with shells and beads around his neck, wrists and ankles, and an arrangement of feathers standing to attention around his head. He led us into a large hut, the walls made of mud and dung, under a thatched roof. Inside, five of his wives were sitting patiently and quietly to one side. The chief's entourage waited for him to be seated and then arranged themselves on the opposite side. The headmaster was given the seat of honour next to the chief, while I hovered around the entrance.

There was a large calabash (a gourd for storing liquid) in the centre of the circle and in turn, each of the men took a sip as they passed it around from one to the next. The last man in the circle offered it to the crew, but when Russell went to pass it to me, they shook their heads. It was apparent that the beer was not on offer to the women, although they were the ones who had brewed the contents.

I did not understand much of the interchange, as along with his assimilation into the life of the local tribes, the headmaster spoke fluent Sotho, and even Russell, being Zulu, was not sure exactly what was going on. I was amused to see that all the men were wearing chain store underpants in a variety of colours, each with a cell phone held in place by knicker elastic around the waist. One of them received a call during the dialogue, but he quickly silenced it.

I was told that the wives were sitting in the correct order from longest married to the most recent one, and they were all dressed exactly the same, with long black skirts, beaded fringed tops which fastened under their arms and the traditional hats which cut close to the head and then flared out like an inverted eggcup.

Russell was unsure at first if he was allowed to film the wives, but as he turned the camera round to face them, no one seemed to mind.

At last the powwow was over and we all crept back out through the low entrance into the sunlight.

Later that afternoon, as we were filming and admiring the school's thriving kitchen garden, we were introduced to a second chief.

"There are two chiefs?" I asked in amazement.

"Yes," replied the headmaster, "our school is right on the border of their territory, so we have pupils from both."

"But isn't it a bit tricky?" I was not quite sure how to put it but our host understood.

"Yes, we have to make sure that we give them equal homage. Even into the 21st century, the word of the local chief is law, and we have to be very tactful."

It was only later I realised how tactful. A few years earlier black children had been admitted to the local mine school, causing a lot of anger among the white parents, so it was decided to move the school into a more rural area.

However the land was already occupied by local market gardeners and they were not happy either.

After weeks of negotiations, they agreed to make space for the school if their remaining land was fenced to prevent the cattle wandering in. They were also assured that the school would provide a lot of extra services, such as the printing of wedding invitations, use of the school hall for functions, sharing a potable water tank, and the installation of pre-paid electricity meters.

The dedication and enthusiasm of this headmaster was something we were to meet time and time again. In conjunction with Rotary he had ISDN lines installed, the school was fully equipped with computers, a well furnished media and TV centre and a well stocked library. He had even encouraged the staff to erect a carport in their spare time and the sports fields would not have disgraced any modern school in the first world.

There is so much that we take for granted in the way most schools are run, but sending out reports, holding parent teacher evenings, sports days and social events in the school for parents and their children, were all quite innovative then. There was an open door policy at many of the schools we visited and this too was a completely new idea for most.

I'm not sure if it's the same today, more than 20 years after independence, but generally speaking, rural African parents do not see any need for preschool education. While we play games with our small children, such as counting steps, teaching different colours and correcting language, school in Africa is seen as the time to learn, and it's the job of those teachers employed to impart all knowledge.

* * *

The following story has nothing to do with my video making, but I would really like to include it, as it gives us more insight into another culture. I had a friend whose maid lived in the *kaya*, or maid's quarters, in the back garden. Although it was not strictly allowed under the law at that time, my friend Susan was happy for her maid's young child to live there too. When the child was old enough to go to school, he was packed off to the nearest one at the beginning of the school year. Susan suggested that the mother go with him, but his mother assured her that was not necessary.

A couple of days later, she realised that she had not seen the child running about and asked where he was. He'd not returned from school, she was told. She immediately jumped into the car and drove around the edge of the nearest township and asked everyone she met if they had seen the missing child. Back home, she printed out dozens of small posters with a picture of the child and her contact details and offered a reward. There was no response.

Susan also worked at the SABC as an announcer, so she arranged for the local black radio stations to broadcast details of the missing child.

Eventually, four weeks later, there was a phone call from a local police station, they had a child who was picked up wandering around the township and was nearly run over. Grabbing her maid, Susan raced over there, and sure enough, there was the young boy looking much the worse for wear. The mother climbed into the back seat of the car, dragging her son after her, and they travelled all the way home in complete silence.

When I first heard this story, quite frankly I didn't believe it.

"Are you sure she never once went to look for him?" I asked.

"Not as far as I know," replied Susan.

"And when you were driving them home in the car she didn't speak to him at all?"

"Not a single word. I was full of questions, wanted to know where he'd been and what he'd been doing, but she just shrugged. It was only a month later that she mentioned that when he tried to enrol, they said he was a year too young to start school and to come back the following January. They told him to go home."

Now I'm sure this is not a typical story, but I did get the impression, over the years I was working out in the rural and not so rural areas, that there was a certain carelessness between some African parents and their children.

8   TALES OUT OF SCHOOL

That first Mpumalanga project we shot for the Provincial Awards took us to another school, but this time it was a high school catering for children from age eleven to eighteen. Their major claim to fame was they had increased the pass rate for the end of school matriculation exams from twenty-six per cent to eight-two per cent which is no mean feat. They also arranged for their pupils to apply for their identity documents which, by law, all citizens of South Africa are required to carry. How I wish they would introduce that worldwide, your South African ID book was used for everything from opening accounts to proving who you were and how old you were.

What blew me away while we were shooting was the notice pinned up in every classroom giving a list of all the transgressions, and their penalty points. These went from attacking and seriously injuring or killing a teacher - ten points, setting fire to the school - nine points, bringing guns and knives to school – eight points, right down to running in the corridors – one point. I just had to ask about it, were they serious? Oh yes, very serious and they had a disciplinary committee which included teachers and pupils who pronounced sentences on all wrongdoers.

The school assembly we attended at the beginning of the day reminded me of those preacher meetings you see on television. The headmaster was soon in full flow, and although I couldn't understand the words, the meaning was very, very clear. Break any rules at your peril. Fire and damnation await all those who do not perform as expected!

It wasn't only the pupils who were to follow the law. In many of the schools there were attendance registers for the teachers too, to make sure they arrived on time or pitched up at all! One proud finalist informed us that, since he had taken over his school, he had stopped all raping of the elder girls by the male staff members. Apparently the previous headmaster and many of the teachers were well known for this kind of behaviour, but no, our informer eagerly told us, he never interfered with the girls and he had stopped his staff from doing it as well. He told us this over and over again.

There was just nothing I could say to that and I thought it wise not to mention this in either the video or the booklet. I simply noted the *'previous'* high levels of crime, how misappropriation of school funds had been stopped and the staff now stayed longer than a couple of terms. I also mentioned the successful 'adopt a cop' scheme.

I did wonder how many cops they had adopted though, as the playground was swarming with them and they appeared to be checking the staff too, as they signed in in the morning. I only hoped that no one would think of relieving them of their weapons and going on the rampage.

I was totally amazed at another school assembly when they had a visiting guest who came to talk to them. As he shuffled towards the podium, the thousand or so high school children went wild, whistling, whooping, clapping and cheering. He must be someone special, a local hero I thought, then watched as two guards in uniform unlocked the handcuffs and the leg irons and in his bright orange prison jumpsuit the guest stood up to address the rapt audience.

What was the message? I wondered. Are they cheering him because he was a gangster and therefore had street cred? Or was this a cultural display towards someone who was stupid enough to get caught? I simply wasn't sure, but the children had made a beautiful banner for him to take back to his cell, inscribed with the words 'Don't do wrong, you will get caught'. I still haven't worked out the mindset at that assembly. Was he a hero or a villain? Many Hollywood or pop stars would be thrilled to experience such a welcome but maybe, in South Africa, you just had to break the law?

I was almost in tears at one primary school in the Northern Cape, which had qualified as a finalist in the Awards that year. It was situated in an area where alcohol dependence was enormously high, and this included many of the pupils as well. Regular school attendance was a big problem, and the staff visited homes to find out why the children were not in the classroom. Often they were out working in the fields harvesting vegetables. Many of the older pupils saw school as childish, since they were kept back year after year and put in the same classes as much younger children. A total of seventy per cent of the children failed to reach high school entrance standards, bringing their education to a halt.

Their playing field was a rough piece of ground, only

kept weed-free by the number of scuffing feet as they played rugby, football and netball in the same space at the same time. All the balls were punctured and deflated, and when we met up with them a few weeks later at the award ceremony, I presented them with new footballs and netballs.

This was poverty at the lowest end, in a school with few resources. The children tended the local cemetery where they had planted 62 trees and they had also created a school garden where they grew their own vegetables. They had negotiated a deal with the local farmer to use his water for their crops in return for feeding his pigs.

The school was situated on an island among the irrigation canals and the headmaster took it in turns to give lifts to a few of the children who walked miles, often barefoot, to and from school each day. For many of them this was their first experience of riding in a car, so it was a great treat.

Many of the parents were illiterate, and I was amused to see, in the mock-up we had of a parent teacher meeting, that one of the mothers attended with her hair in curlers. Was this a sign of status, I wondered?

Another school not too far away had the same problems suffered by many institutions when it came to collecting in the annual school fees. At R20 a year (under £2 or about $3), parents either could not afford this or were unwilling to pay. The staff in this school turned sponsorship sideways and promoted 'adopt a mother', 'adopt a father', and 'adopt a businessman' scheme. This way they collected in a reasonable amount of money, as psychologically it was difficult for the sponsored adults to turn down such an honour and refuse to support the school.

To supplement the funds further, they trained the pupils in gumboot dancing and ballroom dancing and hired the children out for special events, such as weddings, funerals, civic occasions and store openings.

It was astounding what these dedicated teachers were doing to ensure the next generation had a good education. There were two schools back in Mpumalanga Province which I still remember with great fondness. In the first one I was astonished to see the rose bushes and green grass that surrounded all the buildings. The elderly headmistress was dynamite and her staff adored her. Besides teaching, her great love was gardening, but when she first planted the school gardens they were vandalised time and time again.

"What did you do?" I asked her.

She smiled. "I planted them again," she replied.

"And then they left them alone?"

"Oh no, they pulled up all the plants again."

"But that must have been devastating." I was quite shocked.

"But I planted them all again, and again and again, and in the end they gave up and left them to grow. Now, you see, we have beautiful lawns and pretty flowers."

I could only gaze in admiration at her tenacity and her sheer optimism.

Each morning the staff assembled in the headmistress's office for prayers and a hymn, followed by assembly when the children stood outside in rows and listened attentively. There were remedial classes for those who were falling behind, and sign language sessions for the staff to help those few pupils who were deaf. The school had over 800 hundred children, of whom more than 150 were physically and/or mentally challenged.

There was one little boy who had been doing quite well at school until he was involved in a car accident. He was now in a wheelchair, and had suffered brain damage, but this headmistress had fiddled the records and kept him enrolled at her primary school. He was now 17 years old and had just learned to read and write. I recorded a short interview with him for the final shot of the programme and I noticed at the award ceremony several people wiping away the tears.

This deep rural school was also proud of its vegetable garden, not an ordinary one, but a perma-culture garden. As one young lad told us on camera:

"We work hard at this in our extra time and in holidays as it stops us from getting into mischief on the streets!"

We had to stand and listen to a very long extended explanation as to how the vegetables grew, while I was itching to find out why all the classroom doors were riddled with bullet holes. Simple really, they spelt out the name of the school to prevent them being stolen. Now why hadn't I guessed that?

They had also built and stocked a brand new library, costing over a quarter of a million rand, where the older pupils acted out a play about early detection of AIDS. They openly discussed sores on private parts and we got a little uncomfortable as it grew more and more graphic. But it certainly pushed the point home!

The youngest class was also keen to show us their little

song, the words of which said "Don't touch me here, and here and here, if you do I will call the police, one, oh, one, one, one." As they sang, their little hands covered their chests, the tops of their legs, and their small behinds. The rest of the crew were not sure what to make of it but, yet again, I was close to tears.

As if this was not enough to catapult this school into the finals, they also introduced us to a ten year old pupil who had lost everything when the family hut caught fire. The school had rallied around, and found her a new home, new uniform, and made sure she was fed every day.

We had another surprise. Did we know that some of the pupils had earned South African colours in gymnastics? What! From this remote rural school in a very poor area? How had that happened? I'm not sure how a Russian Olympic gymnastics finalist became involved, but she auditioned every child in the school, chose a team and coached those with talent. They gave us a marvellous display to show what they could do. At the end of the session I watched as each child proudly handed back their yellow and purple body suits for safekeeping.

A few kilometres down the road was another school off-the-beaten track, and this time we were not greeted with traditional dancing, but by a whole band of majorettes. Heads held high under white busbies, short red skirts flying, drums beating and batons twirling, they marched in perfect precision. It was not something we ever expected to see way out in the African bush.

This school had a computer centre with over 25 desktops and every child had a lesson each week. They also trooped to the post office on a Tuesday as the headmistress insisted they all open bank accounts to save for the future. I briefly remembered those builders at Cashbuild who could not understand the concept of saving and rioted over the new pension plan. These little ones already understood the idea and even if they only had two cents to pay in, the postmistress was happy to add it to their total.

Just as that thought crossed my mind, I was told that the school had won an art competition from Cashbuild the previous year and spent the ten thousand rand prize on a fresh coat of paint and new rubbish bins. The school was spotlessly clean.

Every time I thought I was beyond being shocked, something unexpected brought me up short. The Indian schools were another such experience. The impression I had at the end of the day's shoot was more of an army boot camp than a school. The children moved with precision, were well drilled and silent in classes even when the teacher was absent.

When we arrived in the morning, one school had prepared a disciplinary hearing, including the parents, members of staff and the headmaster. I assumed that this was a mock-up to show how they handled such matters but no, this was a real case and had been held over from the day before just so we could film it.

"Whatever you do, don't show the boy's face, nor the parents," I whispered in Russell's ear, but I was overheard.

"No, no that's not a problem at all, you can show them all you like," said the headmaster waving his arms in the air.

Was he serious? This child, whatever his offence, did not deserve to be shown in front of an audience of several hundred people, including the premier, half the provincial cabinet, and other notable people, as a wrongdoer being questioned, sentenced and totally demoralised. Even I winced as they drove home his misdemeanours and I decided then and there to devote no more than 20 seconds to this topic.

All the Indian schools we went to had one thing in common, their outstanding ability to raise funds. Activities went from a two cent entrance charge for the weekly 'hair do' competition, to selling a serious number of raffle tickets for major prizes. It was amazing what they achieved, from revamping waste ground into pristine playing fields, to computer centres that rivalled Microsoft head office and, in one location, rebuilding the entire school, after draining the adjoining swamp-land.

While I could admire their achievements, I sensed a frenetic atmosphere in the Indian schools, a driving force to excel but I didn't get the warm, fuzzy feeling I got in the rural schools, where they were making such amazing strides from nothing at all. I had wanted to hug the teacher who grabbed my hand to tell me about the amazing idea she had put into practice.

"I write down lots of things about each child at the end of the year and then I give it to the next teacher to read. Have you ever heard of doing that before? It was all my own idea!"

As I looked at her excited face, I didn't have the heart to tell her it had been a well known practice for decades, even in South Africa. I could only tell her it was a brilliant idea and I was very impressed.

It wasn't only the children who were being educated. We were shown many ABET (Adult Basic Education and Training) classes where adults were being taught to read and write, basic maths, how to budget, and many other simple skills such as using the telephone, or how to check electrical equipment was safe to use.

I'll never forget one scene in a local library where a young boy of about nine years old was teaching his grandfather how to write his own name. The joy on that old man's face as he looked at his very first signature was another occasion when my eyes filled with tears.

After visiting so many schools, (some of them more than once if they were a finalist in different years) and spending time with the children and staff, I felt the whole crew could judge what we were shown and what we noticed by ourselves. Often I would chat with the bed and breakfast owners as well, to get a feel for the area, and learn a little about the background of the tribal chiefs, and anything else that might be useful.

So when we met up with a lady from Scandinavia who was, I think, doing some kind of community work and research, I invited her to come along on the shoot the following day to the school which had reached the finals.

Early next morning she squeezed into the crew car and off we drove, through a smart village, to the newly fenced school where the children were waiting to greet us with a song. We were shown how they were given breakfast, and then lunch before they went home and some of their amazing art work which included models of rockets, a working radio and a remote controlled bicycle.

We learned the school acted as the local post office and they were proud of their parent teacher relationships. All good stuff, and I wasn't surprised they had also impressed the judges.

In the meantime our European visitor had wandered off to explore the rest of the school and we only met up again in the late afternoon as we were packing the gear back into the car.

"Oh, those poor, poor children!" she exclaimed. "They are so poor, they have nothing. We should arrange to collect money for them!"

"It's really not necessary," I replied.

"How can you say that, look at how they are fed at school, their parents are too poor to buy food for them." She was really beginning to get on my nerves.

"You are comparing this semi-rural area in Africa with urban living in northern Europe, right?"

"Yes, and look at the small houses they have to live in, such a shame."

I told Aarnav to stop the car. "Come and look at this," I said as I helped her out from the back seat and walked to the side of the road.

"See that sports stadium? It's brand new. Also over there, you will see a community hall, also new. How many children did you notice today who were barefoot?"

"Well they all had shoes, but..."

"It's the first rural school we've visited in nine years where every child wore proper shoes. What you didn't know is that this area is tribal land, like most other rural areas, and this community owns a diamond mine."

Our visitor's eyes grew large. "No!" she exclaimed.

"Yes, they do, and it's very profitable. They don't work it themselves, but employ a team of French miners, and every week De Beers or Anglo American fly a plane in to collect the rough diamonds they've brought to the surface."

"Have you been to a squatter camp and seen real poverty?" I continued. She shook her head.

We'd seen an informal settlement on the way into the nearby town and Aarnav suggested we could show her what poor really was.

I felt rather sorry for this kind lady when she saw the conditions in the squatter camp. No toilets, no running water, kids more than half naked, and rubbish, rubbish everywhere with mangy dogs scavenging in the heaps of discarded detritus.

The lady was appalled. She gazed in horror at the scene, she'd had absolutely no idea. I guess it was not really that surprising as visitors were rarely shown the worst of any town or city, the areas that are known to be dangerous and unwelcoming to strangers. Usually we never went into townships unless we were with a respected member of the community, and I was always grateful that I did not have an all-white team, Russell and Aarnav blended in much better. I often laughed and said that I must be the only white face for miles in any direction so they had better take good care of me.

We had a big problem in one school we went to. They had not qualified for the finals, but the nominee was just one lady who taught in this rural high school. This was the first of only two occasions we featured an individual. Our subjects were always departments, or institutions, but her work had been so outstanding the judges had wanted to recognise her selfless devotion.

We arrived just after seven in the morning to capture shots of the pupils arriving at school and I had the rest of the day all mapped out in my mind. We would interview the lady, show her teaching in the classroom, record a few sound bites, a short sentence from some of the children she had counselled, a comment from the headmaster and general shots of the school. I knew exactly what I wanted.

I hadn't taken into account what the school wanted.

I groaned when I saw several large, black cars (BMWs and Mercedes) draw up outside the school gates.

"Oh Lord," I complained to Russell and Aarnav, "here come the dignitaries. "We must shoot round them, they are not part of the programme at all. Please don't let us get bogged down with long speeches and praise singers."

We managed to grab our heroine and herd her into one of the empty classrooms and she told us how she had helped many of the troubled children and persuaded them not to commit suicide, and how she got practical help for them. She was relaxed and easy in front of the camera like so many Africans, and we got off to a good start.

Walking back outside I saw with dismay that a large stage had been set up at one end of the playground which was now buzzing with important people, including the local chief, and I guessed some councillors and other figureheads. Our heroine appeared a few minutes later and was called up onto the stage. Much to my horror, I noticed she had changed clothes, and was in a totally different outfit to the one we had just recorded. Remember the continuity problem?

I decided that I would feature this part briefly, as a local tribute to her from the community and then persuade her to change back again while we showed her day to day work.

The speeches went on and on and on, followed by several dancing groups, followed by more speeches and then a choir materialized from behind the toilet block and sang several songs which were never ending.

I was beginning to fret, as I *had* to complete this shoot in one day. We were booked at the next location on the following day, which was a Saturday, for a sports initiative, and that was 300 kilometres away. This school would close in a few hours, and I'd only filmed one interview so far.

In desperation, I grabbed the attention of one of the bigwigs at the side of the stage and explained the problem. He looked quite startled, and really could not understand why I did not want to show the celebrations and so on. What was more, as soon as the performances were over, we were all going to eat, the women had been cooking all week, he was sure we were going to enjoy the food.

I have to confess this was one of those times when I lost a bit of my cool and decided to ignore the ceremonial proceedings and go ahead with the shoot the way it should be. I arranged for our heroine to leave the stage, and gently frogmarched her into the nearest classroom which, to my horror was empty.

"Where are all the chairs and desks?" I asked.

"They are out in the playground for the celebrations," I was told.

"Then bring back at least twelve desks and chairs, and I need twelve children as well, drag them in, and I want you," I pulled my heroine by the arm, "to stand here and teach them."

"What shall I...?"

"It doesn't matter, anything, just pretend. I will use the words from the interview we have, over the pictures of you teaching. We need to show what you do every day. Can you do that for us?"

To my relief our heroine understood what we wanted and she was very cooperative, and played her part to perfection.

Refusing all but a bite of the enormous feast that had been laid on for us, our finalist took us to see where one of her pupils lived in the adjacent township. It was a one room shack with the bare essentials. Both the boy's parents had died of AIDS and at fourteen he was living on his own. He was still attending school and working after hours, not only to feed himself, but to save up enough money to reunite his two younger sisters, who had been fostered out. His goal was to pass his Matric, or school leavers' exam, and get the family back together again.

Next our selfless teacher took us to see a local businessman she had bullied, (her words) into helping those children who came to her with their problems. We were also lucky to talk to a young girl who admitted that she would have taken her own life had it not been for her teacher, who had given her a reason to live.

But the most amazing interview was with one of the

parents. She was short, and her face was so deeply wrinkled it was almost impossible to guess her age. Her clothes were faded and frayed and her shoes had been fashioned from cast -off tyres. She had problems standing upright but she was very keen to tell us about her son. She began to talk fast even before we had plugged in the microphone and tested the levels, so we had to ask her to start again. Off she went a dozen words a second until she literally ran out of breath. I asked Russell what she'd said.

"She says that her son did well at school, and he passed his Matric with very high marks and now he has gone away to university in another town. The lady here organised it all for her and she is so proud. No one in her family, and no one in the whole township, including all the important people in this area, has ever gone to a university before. He is the very first one. She is very, very proud."

"Wow, yes she must be! What university is he at? And what is he studying?" Russell turned to ask the small wizened mother, and they spoke for a couple of minutes.

"She doesn't know which town, or which university, or what he is learning or what work he will do afterwards, she only knows that his teacher organised it all and found the money for his fees and he has been gone now two years."

"Oh..." I wasn't sure what to say. Two years? I wondered if he would ever come back to this rural backwater, but maybe that was not the point, he had made his mother the proudest lady in the area, and he would have undreamed of opportunities for his future.

We finally had all the footage we needed to show our heart-warming story, now all we had to do was say goodbye and extract ourselves gracefully from the scene. It would be totally unforgivable in African culture not to thank the chief and the headmaster and just disappear. Once again, our switched-on heroine smoothed the path for us.

"I have to be in Nelspruit by seven o'clock, as I have arranged an interview for this pupil," she announced, dragging one of the larger boys into the group, "and these kind people have offered me a lift. If we hurry now, we can make it in time."

We had? I gasped, the crew car was only just big enough for the three of us, our cases and all the gear, and we were heading off in the opposite direction, but there was nothing I could say. With a great deal of difficulty, we all squeezed into the vehicle, passengers buried beneath camera, lights and sound equipment and we set off to drive 300 kilometres in the opposite direction. We left behind a large crowd who watched us in amazement and then, I heard later, continued to party well into the night. I suspect we were not hugely missed.

By the time we rocked up at the sports centre the following morning, we needed matchsticks to keep our eyes open. Thank goodness the next day was Sunday, which might give us a few hours to catch our breath and log the shots, collate the pictures and write the script for both projects. I calculated I could allow myself maybe half an hour of relaxation before we began again on the Monday morning.

I had thought this next insert was purely a sports' initiative but I was wrong. It also included Hantam dancing, a cross-over between Bushman and Afrikaans culture, with traditional music played on instruments I had never seen before.

We were then taken to one of the houses in the nearby township and seated in the best chairs while a variety of weirdly dressed people began to talk to us in a very strange way. I began at first to feel very uncomfortable and then quite frightened and, at the first opportunity, I made our apologies and a rapid escape.

"What was that all about?" I asked Russell as we drove off. "Did you see how they behaved? It was so scary, I wondered if they were about to attack us!"

"I doubt it," he replied. "They were acting out a traditional play."

"Oh." Not for the first time, I felt very stupid and very ignorant. I had even suggested to Russell in a quiet whisper that maybe he should not record the strange scene, but luckily he had rolled the camera anyway.

On the lighter side, in another school, the teacher and children were all ready and waiting for us as we negotiated the breeze block steps into her Portakabin classroom.

She smiled brightly at us and the children, aged around nine years, all turned to say "Good morning visitors from television!" They were all excited and couldn't wait to show off what they knew.

"Now," began the teacher, "who can tell me who is the most famous person in South Africa?" Hands shot up like a forest.

"Our chief," several chorused in unison. The teacher's face fell.

"No, I'm thinking of someone who lives a little further away."

"Mr Mangope, our headmaster," cried out one bright spark.

The teacher began to look a little frazzled, were our cameras recording this?

"No, now take your time and think carefully. This very, very important man lives a long, long way away in Johannesburg, the capital." Unfortunately the capital of South Africa is not Johannesburg, but we didn't like to mention this.

The children sat there, puzzled looks on their faces, they didn't have a clue, so the teacher put them out of their misery. "It's Nelson Mandela!" she announced with a big smile, but still the children sat there, staring at her blankly.

"Who is he?" one brave soul asked after several minutes of total silence.

This would make great television, I thought, but that was not my job. I walked to the front of the class and suggested we start over on a different topic and the teacher's relieved face was all the thanks I needed.

On other occasions, as an ex-teacher I would wince, especially in the English classes we interrupted, as I heard information passed on that I knew was incorrect, but good manners and my respect for those underpaid educators kept me silent.

One location we went to film in the Western Cape, just outside Cape Town, was to highlight a finalist that ran a service for schools and schoolchildren called 'The Safe Schools Project'. We had seen high mesh fences round many of the educational establishments, (even those in the white urban areas were protected and had guards on the gates) but never anything like this. I doubt the average prison has tighter security. Above the ten foot linked chain fences were rolls of razor wire and, if you got through this, every window was covered with a thick metal grill plus more barbed wire.

We were also shown the infrared sensors on the walls, the panic buttons and they arranged for the children to give us a demonstration on how they responded when the alarms went off. We were also to witness the prompt arrival of the armed response vehicles which drove into the school grounds within minutes.

"But why?" I asked. "You don't have really expensive equipment here do you? Why would people want to break in, even during the day when everyone is around to see them?" I really couldn't understand it at all.

But theft was *not* the main problem.

"It's the gangs. If a fight breaks out then they think nothing of shooting across the school grounds, even at playtime when the kids are out there. Did you notice the intercom at the gate?"

"Yes."

"It's manned all day, and we are going to show you what happens when we set off the alarm, and how the children have been trained to evacuate quickly and assemble in the safest places."

This was the darker side of Africa. How could any gangster think of shooting across a crowded playground? And what was worse, we also learned that school territory was often used for drug dealing, frequently involving the children as sellers. This was quite deliberate, as offenders under the age of sixteen could not be prosecuted, so they were ideal candidates for carrying illegal substances. In the worst case scenario, they would be released from police custody and sent back home.

It was an uphill battle for those educating these youngsters. Often the local heroes and role models in the townships were the drug dealers, the car hijackers and the villains. Why work 40 hours a week labouring in an office, a shop, a factory or even on the land, when you could pick up twice as much money through crime in only a couple of hours? It's difficult to refute that argument, especially when you see how the gang members paraded round the streets dressed in the latest fashions, swaggering with their high tech ghetto blasters, and 'pulling' every girl in sight. If there was no shame in crime, if in fact it heightened your celebrity status, what was the point of aspiring to a career and a boring everyday sort of life?

What was more, if you were caught, then going to prison, often referred to as 'going home', gave you time with your mates, a roof over your head, free food, television, minimal work and a well maintained gym.

The schools in these violent townships had their own mediation and counselling centres for both staff and pupils, and they also formed cluster groups to exchange ideas on how to stay safe. They arranged day trips for the children to non-violent areas and there were attempts to negotiate with the gang leaders, to persuade them that schools were 'no go' areas for everyone's sake.

The Safe Schools Project also had a call centre in the middle of Cape Town and, even in the couple of hours we were there, the six operators were constantly answering the dozens of calls that came in. The phones were ringing off the hook. There was a free number for children to use as a life line, someone to talk to, to tell a friendly voice of their sad home lives invaded by drugs, violence and alcohol. As we tried to film, we were constantly interrupted by the phones ringing, and our interviewees breaking off to answer them.

"We must answer these calls as quickly as possible," one explained to us. "We have to be here for them. Often they cannot stay long in the phone box, or they are scared of being seen, or they have borrowed a cell phone and must give it back very quickly." The operator rattled off a list of reasons why he had to break off and answer yet another ringing phone.

Not far away, on the other side of the city, we filmed in a unit set up in a major hospital for traumatised children and families. The entrance was a copy of a Disneyland Castle and here the children were welcomed and reassured that no bad people could ever, ever, go beyond that point. It was almost surreal to turn the corner in an ordinary hospital and come face to face with a floor-to-ceiling fairy tale castle, complete with painted doors and a portcullis. Ducking down to walk in, there were doors on either side of the corridor, each on a different theme, a mock-up kitchen, a lounge, a playroom, and the *pièce de résistance*, a fantasy room with life-sized toy soldiers and moving Disney characters against a background of lively, yet soothing music.

This whole area was completely safe and I have no words for the dedication of the people who dealt with children as young as three or four who had often been sexually molested and raped. They gave them one-on-one attention, talking, reassuring, and probing the truth in such a way as not to cause any further trauma.

A rumour had started a few years earlier, that having sex with a virgin protected you from getting AIDS and, if you were already HIV, then it would also cure you. What better way to ensure you chose a virgin than to pick a very young child? The idea was just too appalling, but like a plague, the idea spread and I was told only the very worst cases were reported in the press.

In five years this centre had treated up to nineteen thousand children. Some had already been in the hospital long term, as a result of being subjected to scenes of violence, or physical and mental injuries at home.

While it was heart-warming to see the unit and learn about what these wonderful people do, it was horrific to know there was such a need for it. Yet another day's shoot when it would have been just too easy to break down in tears.

In another location we were introduced to many young children who suffered from alcohol foetal syndrome, caused by the huge quantities of alcohol imbibed by their mothers while pregnant. This led to many mental problems, and in one school there was a special unit to help these little ones who had not had a good start in life. It was doubtful, even with the extra teaching, if they would ever function normally, they were already scarred for life, even before they were born.

You got tough when you went into poor areas, familiarisation could deaden the senses to some degree, but you came to notice those who were trying to help themselves, those who were prepared to work hard, to spend or save even pennies wisely, to make sacrifices to get a good education or obtain a job.

So when you saw people who just sat back and whined about how hard life was, you did have less sympathy for them. This might not have been fair, but it's only human to compare one group with another. I still find it hard to relate to children in first world countries who try to avoid school, and duck out of classes. They have no idea how privileged they are. I've seen tiny tots walk miles barefoot, next to main roads and across open country, to attend school. Even at this young age, they knew that education was the passport out of poverty.

9   HOSPITALS, HEALING & AIDS

Every provincial government is made up of several different departments, such as roads, schools, transport, cost centre and so on. So when the scheme for 'service excellence' rolled around each year, more and more departments entered. There was a lot of prestige in winning the trophy, and some provinces even introduced cash incentives for the winners.

So it was inevitable that among the nominees we were asked to film each year, to show how they had improved and what they were doing to put the people first, were hospitals and clinics. Lots of them.

I was dreading this, I hate hospitals with a passion. From very early days when I ignominiously fainted in my first biology lesson I have loathed, in no particular order, the sight of needles, blood, saline drips and operating theatres. It was no good me hiding behind Russell and pushing him in front to film the gory bits, I would still have to look at these images when logging the shots and stare at them again in edit.

Perhaps it was greed, or just pure professionalism, but I decided there was no way round it. I would have to go in with my eyes wide open where before I had only ever entered such places with my eyes screwed tightly shut, opening them only to peer every now and again at the floor to see where I was going. For me, this was like walking over red hot coals, and I was trembling as we entered our first place of healing. I still had nightmares about the day I spent in the operating theatre in Johannesburg when I pretended to watch the cataract operation.

However, the first hospital we went to was for psychiatric and TB patients in Durban. We were amazed to learn that it had nearly eight hundred beds and was run by a dynamic person we were to meet many times in the nine years we filmed these projects. It was also amazing that none of us in the crew had ever heard of this hospital, although it was in our own home town, and we even got lost trying to find it.

Housed in dingy, red-brick buildings, at the back of an industrial area, we were surprised to find the rooms light and airy, and even though there was no chance of the small TB patients ever recovering, there was still an atmosphere of cheerfulness. I do remember that each child had a small teddy bear, collected by a charity, and every time we saw one of the children, tiny hands clutched the leg or arm of their personal bear.

Up on the Reef (the area around Pretoria and Johannesburg) I had discovered that often it was difficult to film people as we would be met with grumbles about how we were making money out of their situation. They were happy to appear on camera and role play for us, but they demanded an appearance fee and a few of them got quite aggressive about it. Of course our budget never extended to such luxuries, so I hit on the idea of buying brightly coloured plastic bowls and buckets and using these as currency, it worked a treat.

While we were away on location, we could hardly traipse round with piles of bulky kitchenware, so I decided to buy lollipops instead. These became hugely popular, with both children and adults. It always caused a laugh when I offered them their 'actors' fees', and the sweets were also useful in places like hospitals if there were no dietary problems. This out of the way TB hospital was the perfect place to hand out lollipops, and after our visit, I had to seriously restock. But at a couple of cents per sweet, it didn't break the bank!

Over the years we filmed several times in Durban's largest state hospital, situated right on the beachfront, as they crept further and further up the list from bronze, to silver to finally win the gold trophy. A few years before I had actually been incarcerated in there myself, and I appreciated the work that they did. The huge crowds of the sick and the lame were quite intimidating. I'd not really been aware of my surroundings when I had been in there as a patient, now I was looking at it with very different eyes.

In the accident and emergency department there were people with stab wounds and gunshot wounds, streaming with blood, and several of the women were weeping and wailing. Many of the waiting patients sat in silence, they simply looked beaten and world weary – on the point of giving up.

I was beginning to despair that we could make such scenes look good until I met the lady in charge. She was dynamite, and a brilliant example to her staff. She had introduced so many new things, such as a hospital radio service, the in-house magazine, an equipment sharing pool, regular fire drills, a complaints procedure, thank you cards for the staff, an induction course for new staff; the list went on and on.

I saw a row of T-shirts hanging on a line in one of the halls. They were inscribed with heartbreaking messages about the abuse children had suffered at the hands of family and friends. I asked about them, I wanted to know why they were strung out across the waiting area.

"The children we get in here as the result of physical abuse have been encouraged to write their thoughts on the T-shirts," the lady in charge told me. "Then we hang them where everyone can see them. It helps to make everyone aware of the problem. We hope it will help stop some of the abuse."

There was something new to learn every day.

If I thought there were enormous crowds in the city hospital, I was not prepared for the ones we filmed in the Indian areas. Hundreds and hundreds of ailing people sat patiently waiting their turn to see the doctor, standing up and moving along a seat each time the patient at the front of the queue was called forward. The doctors told us they were allocated three minutes for each person, and very few were even taken into the examining room. It was not unusual to wait for as many as eight hours to be seen, and often it meant a return visit the next day to collect the medicine.

Despite the overcrowding in many of these hospitals, the dedicated staff had solved the shortage of pillows by making more themselves using their own funds, and marking the sheets with the name of the hospital to control theft. They had also hived off staff or brought in volunteers to give informal talks on hygiene and family planning. I was particularly taken with a huge poster which showed how having a large family split the resources and produced thin, sick children in comparison to a small family that could feed, clothe and educate their healthier offspring.

When health departments situated in the rural areas were nominated and short-listed in the awards, we were constantly reminded that many of the parents were both illiterate and unemployed, and there was a constant battle to encourage something as basic as breast-feeding. Using cow's milk in baby bottles (which were unwashed and unsterilized), was seen as a sign of status, and first world behaviour. This led to many cases of diarrhoea and so the staff introduced a drive to persuade mothers to give their babies lots to drink. The traditional way to stop loose bowels in Africa is not to offer the babies anything at all. We saw many demonstrations where the nurse would pour water into clay pots full of holes. You could see the water running out, but the sponge inside became wet and some water was retained in the bottom of the pot. In this way they hoped to show that it was vitally important not to dehydrate babies and children.

I learned that while the pharmaceutical companies produced expensive re-hydration medication, it was simple and cheap to make this yourself at home using clean, boiled water, salt and sugar. The staff even produced double-ended spoons, one small spoon for the salt and a large spoon at the other end to measure out the sugar.

The crew were a bit stunned the first time we were taken into a room where a row of mothers were all having breastfeeding lessons. You could see this sometimes in the streets, but you tended to look away. You most certainly didn't stare at the naked breasts. Now we were being urged not only to look, but record them on camera too. Even though his skin was dark, I could see that Russell's face was a bright red.

Every effort was made to make hospitals warm and friendly, especially the neonatal departments. It was vital that new mothers were persuaded to return at regular intervals to have their newborns weighed and checked. Often these new mothers had only come to have their babies in the hospital in the first place, because there had been complications in the pregnancy. At least their confinement took place in clean and clinical surroundings, but these babies especially, needed to be checked to ensure they were developing normally.

Many of the hospitals showed us the 'kangaroo' practice they had introduced, where the naked baby was placed on mother's bare chest, and then both were wrapped together in a blanket. This helped mother and baby to bond, and was a great comfort to the babies. It reminded me of the time I had played in the Mediterranean Sea with my eldest as a small child. That close, intimate contact had opened a well of maternal feeling that never left me and it's one of my most vivid memories.

It's traditionally African to carry your baby on your back. I tried this once with my first offspring. Great idea, I thought, it leaves both your hands free. But I never got the knack of it. I would sit on the bed and copy the exact movements I'd seen performed by the local women, but each time I tried to stand up, something would unravel and my daughter would tumble off onto the bed before I was even vertical. I could never work out what I was doing wrong but she landed flat on her back behind me every time. I gave up and used the pushchair.

There is a problem with carrying babies on your back, especially if it goes on for a long time. Apart from the custom of grabbing the child by one arm and swinging it around like a flag, it can distort eyesight, as the baby will have its head turned to one side, usually the same side and this can cause visual problems later.

In all our many hospital visits, I was struck by the simple, but effective ideas we saw being put into practice. Coloured footprints and lines leading to different departments for those who couldn't read, low tables for wheelchairs when forms needed to be filled in, bright murals on the walls and in the wards, and all-hours visiting a vital service for families who had travelled miles and miles to come and comfort their sick relatives.

Our visits to places of healing, especially the hospitals and clinics in the predominantly Indian areas, were not havens of peace and quiet. Often there were more relations than patients as they crowded noisily around the beds, forcing the doctors and nurses to push their way through to attend their charges.

Some hospitals arranged an adoption service with people in the community, who would supervise the daily taking of medication, especially for those discharged patients suffering from TB. There was a tendency to either stop taking the pills as soon as you felt better, or share them out with friends and family.

I was amazed to see patients, their drip poles beside them, sitting out on the grass, and little TB patients five years and younger being pulled along in a linen trolley, or walking crocodile-fashion to and from the dining area. They would never leave the hospital, but the staff still organised play and learning centres to keep them occupied and amused.

We caused an awful fuss in one rural hospital where they were keen to show us how they used the staff van to take patients home if the ambulance wasn't available. Two nurses rushed inside, while we set up the camera in the car park and waited. Eventually, the nurses reappeared with a lady whose legs had been amputated. They were puffing, panting and sweating profusely as they carried her slung between them like a sack of potatoes.

"We are going to have to do this in one take," I hissed. "They will never make it out a second time."

All went well. The patient was loaded into the van without being dropped, and Russell hopped on board for some inside shots while we followed behind in the crew car. At the other end the nurses went through the same procedure, sweating buckets as they offloaded their very large patient, despite the fact she was missing two limbs, and struggled through the narrow doorway into a nearby house. We popped inside as well to record the patient sitting in a comfortable chair, smiling, with a cup of tea in her hand. I thought we made the point nicely.

We all went back to the hospital to record the staff choir and other innovative ideas, and it was only several hours later that there was a frantic cell phone call to the subject specialist who was conducting us round. Apparently there was a very irate man at the front gate demanding to know why two nurses had driven into *his* yard four hours ago, dumped a total stranger with no legs in the best chair in *his* front room, handed her *his* cup of tea and driven off again. Even Matron had difficulty in keeping a straight face as she rushed off to pour oil on troubled waters and arrange to have the patient returned to hospital. We just collapsed in fits of laughter.

There was another incident that was not the slightest bit funny and it is one I am very ashamed of. We were in Durban in a hospital that had been built for black Africans and I was told it was the place to ask the ambulance to take you if you'd been shot, as the staff there were whizzes with gunshot and stab wounds. It was a very hot day, we were tired and frazzled and trying to get a sound bite from this lady who wanted to tell us about the excellent treatment she'd received from the staff. She had regained her sight for the first time in 60 years, and they were teaching her how to walk, also for the first time. It was a very moving story, and she was only too thrilled to share it with us.

We tried this four times, but on each take, we were interrupted halfway through by loud wailing. I stormed off into the next ward determined to stop the noise and saw a woman standing in the archway about to scream again.

"Look, please will you just stop that for one moment!" I said "I am trying to film next door and..."

I got no further, because she thrust a bundle at me and fell back onto the nearest bed. I looked down. Inside the blanket I was holding in my arms was a baby. It was cold, stiff and very obviously dead. I stood frozen to the spot and I felt the blood rise in my cheeks. How could I have been so crass, so selfish, and so thoughtless? I gulped and gently handed back the small, lifeless child.

"I'm so sorry," I mumbled as I backed out of the ward, bumping into one of the nurses who came up behind me. Yes, there was silence then, and I got my sound bite, but the feeling of shame has stayed with me ever since.

But I was not going to be able to avoid the gory stuff indefinitely. The cardio specialist hospital was one place I always dreaded visiting, even though we were greeted by the same manager who had run the TB clinic a couple of years earlier. He insisted we watched the procedures on their state of the art equipment. Everyone else was fascinated watching the dye run around inside living patients wired up like a space station, but I was propping myself against the nearest wall counting the cracks in the ceiling which refused to keep still.

The wound clinic near Johannesburg was a bit of a problem too. The whole department consisted of only one room, and I was at my wit's end as to how I was going to create a five minute film featuring three posters and a bookshelf. I asked Russell to film one of the trolleys topped by a small metal cover passing by the door, thinking it would make an extra cutaway shot, until I was told it was yet another baby on its way to the morgue. Maybe wise not to include that.

At a large hospital in Pietermaritzburg, for the third time, we ran into the same dynamic manager who had moved on from the TB hospital to the cardio hospital and was now in charge of the state hospital in the provincial capital. Once again, he had worked wonders at raising the service standards, including a new treatment for curing leg ulcers in the elderly. It worked, and I am not sure why it hasn't been copied elsewhere, as we interviewed the patient in the last stages of his successful treatment.

Another hospital department had reached the finals, and I groaned when I saw it was the operating theatre. This was the ultimate challenge for me, and they tried to persuade us all to go and watch a caesarean section. I said that I thought there was a terrible risk of infection, the best excuse I could come up with, and sent Russell in, along with the expectant father. It's a totally new idea in Africa to allow the dad to attend the birth, and I only saw any evidence of this in one hospital.

It's a sad fact that many men will walk out on a girlfriend as soon as they know she is pregnant or, sometimes, hang around for a year or so and then vanish. The burden of having to provide for a family as well as their own needs could appear overwhelming. The vast numbers of women I met in all the years I was filming were single mothers struggling to cope, often with several young children. I had to admire these women, as they battled the odds to feed, clothe and educate the next generation. Grandmothers helped where they could, but in a society where it was usual to produce children before marriage, the responsibility fell heavily on the maternal parent.

I remember a scene we encountered when we went into one office. There were three women all screaming and shouting, each attempting to make her voice the loudest. It appeared they had all come to claim the widow's pension of a recently deceased employee. We were told the newly departed had married two of the women, while the third had produced three children with him previously. Each lady was convinced she had the strongest claim and was quite determined to prove it, and verbally too, as there was little official documentation to back up any of their claims. I felt sorry for the manager who was trying to sort out the problem and thankfully left him to it as we ducked out and went to find a quieter office to set up the cameras.

Back in the hospital, to take my mind off the gruesome scene and in an effort to squash my squeamishness, I asked Russell to lie on the trolley with the camera and point it at the ceiling, while I arranged for him to be wheeled along the corridor.

"You want me to do what?" he asked in amazement.

"Just lie down and we will pretend you are being taken in for an operation." He looked at me in alarm. "I want to show it from the patient's point of view, and we'll say that at every stage the staff members are helpful and friendly and so on."

He very reluctantly climbed on, petrified that something would go wrong, while I asked a nurse to lean over and ask if he was all right.

"I am fine," Russell protested. "You're not going to d-d-do, anything to me are y-y-you?" he stuttered, thoroughly alarmed.

"No, just wheel you along the corridor," I reassured him. Afterwards, I'm not sure I saw anyone leap off a trolley so fast. He was still shaking a little half an hour later.

One of the most heart-warming places we went to was a small community hospital out in the middle of nowhere, and I mean that, it was 50 kilometres from the nearest town. The staff had petitioned all three cell phone companies in South Africa asking them to erect a mast so they could get coverage, that's how isolated they were. Patients arrived on foot, by bicycle, in carts and in wheelbarrows.

They gave us one of the warmest welcomes we had ever received. They showed us the vegetable garden tended by the long-term and permanent patients, the room where they taught those workers who could neither read nor write, and assembled the choir who sang beautifully for us.

Inevitably the subject of AIDS came up and I asked if they had any idea how prevalent it was in this deep rural area; it was not a notifiable disease in South Africa.

"As you know, we are not allowed to test for AIDS, even with the patients' permission, but for our own information, and to help protect our staff..." Our hostess paused. "Put it this way, we '*suspect*' one hundred per cent of all our expectant mothers have AIDS."

We were shocked, *every* mother to be? But what about the campaign to persuade the men to wear condoms? We'd seen many a demonstration where health workers peeled condoms over the ends of bananas or cucumbers, much to the amusement of their audience.

"The men use that as a weapon. If the women ask them to use condoms, the answer is 'no,' it's seen as not manly. Men like it skin to skin and won't have anything else." It was a stark reminder that, despite the number of female government ministers in parliament, the women in rural Africa were still second class citizens.

This small hospital scrimped and scraped with the little funding they received, but their hospitality was overwhelming and they put on a fabulous lunch for us.

Food was often a problem on a shoot. Each evening we would buy a packed lunch from a nearby supermarket for the next day and we ate while we worked. We never stopped for a meal in the day, there was never enough time.

When we were fed by our hosting department, we would often forget to eat the packed lunch which I would then find several days later, under the car seat or in the boot, now green, furry and beyond repair. I particularly remember some meat bought by one of the crew members which he simply refused to throw away, until it practically jumped out of the car all by itself when the smell got too bad.

Each evening we would take it in turns to choose where to eat. As he was an Indian, Aarnav always chose a curry house, I went for Italian and Russell herded us into the nearest steak house. Africans love their meat.

Perhaps I'm biased and too European, but a lot of African cooking does not appeal to me. I remember one rural shoot on a weekend when I was working with my equipment partner Brian. It took us over an hour to find this small rural village down a deeply rutted grass track.

We parked up and got the gear out of the car and went to meet the client. I think it was a celebration of the opening of a new classroom at the local school, remember, any excuse is a good excuse for a party.

They walked us over the playing fields, simply an open piece of ground and showed us where the lunch was being prepared. To our dismay, we saw them slit the throats of a couple of desperately sad cows, then hack them into pieces and drop these into a huge cauldron of boiling water where their forlorn eyes gazed at us as they floated on the greasy water.

We gazed at each other in horror. It was extremely rude to refuse food, and we were not sure how we were going to get out of this one. To our enormous relief, that was the fare for the huddled masses sitting out under the boiling African sun. When the honoured guests arrived in their fleet of black limousines, complete with bodyguards sporting Ray-Ban shades, the dignitaries were ushered into the cool of the shaded tents, and we discovered they had prepared a more normal repast for us in the local school. We breathed a sigh of relief.

I marvelled once again at the innate patience of the rural African, content to sit out in the open for hours waiting for the chiefs and other notable people to arrive. They accepted that. Shaded tents with chairs were provided for the top brass, but they were only worthy of a roped off area and sat on the bare, hard earth. No one seemed to mind, they knew their place, and it was presumably enough they would receive a free meal.

I learned to lie very convincingly and pretended I was allergic to chicken heads (called beaks) and claws, boiled almost to extinction, and suspicious pieces of meat swimming in fat, and always made a beeline for the salads, sadza and mealie meal, two variations of the African maize meal porridge.

We did make a big mistake once in the Northern Cape. I'd not been aware that they grew so many grapes in that part of the country, and when I tried them they were sweet, juicy and very tasty. Seeing we enjoyed them, our hosts that day insisted on giving us huge quantities of them and, as we drove away all smiles, we ate one after another. Yes, I'm sure you are way ahead of me here. Too much fruit in too short a time leads to a desperate need to visit the smallest room in the house. But we were out on location, miles from any conveniences, and in desperation, I was forced to knock on a stranger's door to ask if I could visit her bathroom. Even the medicine I carried with me at all times was not enough to counteract the effect of so many grapes.

In another province the finalist team we went to film worked in a local clinic known for its outreach programme. They took us to a house where a lady was dying of AIDS. It was a small mud hut, housing only one bed, a chair and a kitchen hotplate balanced on a cardboard box. It was dark inside, but light enough to see the appalling sores on this poor lady's face. She just lay in that bed day after day, staring at the wall waiting to die. The only contact she had was the with health visitor who came daily to dress her wounds and bring her food. At the award ceremony later that month, we heard she was *late* as the Africans say, and I was glad her suffering was over.

In those early days there was a lot of stigma about contracting AIDS and it wasn't until several years had passed, and local celebrities, well known actors and musicians 'came out' and told everyone why they were sick, that it became more acceptable. Most often the women were blamed for infecting the men, which was grossly unfair as very few of the rural women would ever have much opportunity of being unfaithful. In the meantime, their partners were away in the big cities, often working on the mines, where they so often sought solace with other ladies, or even had a second family.

A local film-maker won many awards for his story of a rural woman forced to build a separate hut away from the village after being ostracised for infecting her husband. They believed if you went near anyone with AIDS you would catch it as well and, despite the huge campaign using all the media to explain how it was passed on from one to another, it took a long time to make any inroads into the prevalent mindset.

Another huge problem with telling anyone you had AIDS was that no insurance company, often associated with the workplace, would pay out for death by AIDS. Of course the problem was made worse when the information got out that 'AIDS does not kill you,' and it circulated like wildfire. This statement is true, the disease only facilitates death by destroying your body's defences against other germs and viruses. So AIDS was never written on the death certificate as the cause of death, but there were always those only too happy to tell everyone the real reasons and this could invalidate the payouts.

We were not always impressed with our finalists though. One health district expected us to film them in their offices, but I explained it was necessary to show them actively at work, visiting their clinics, and liaising with their staff and maybe a patient or two. I could understand they were unwilling to leave their air-conditioned offices and traipse for miles in the heat on a very hot day in the northern Karoo. However, that was not the real reason for their reluctance. After driving around for almost an hour, I suddenly realised that they were lost, they did not know where the clinics were, and when we eventually stumbled into one, the staff there hadn't the faintest idea who these people were, or that they were finalists in an award scheme! If we were embarrassed, our finalist team were totally unashamed, as they chattered away to the clinic staff, introducing themselves and making comments on everything they saw, while we dutifully filmed all the right procedures and kept our less than admiring thoughts to ourselves.

They did however know there was a container out on one of the main roads, fully equipped to test the passing truck drivers for AIDS and where they handed out literature and advice to long distance hauliers. This has been a major cause of the rapid spread of AIDS on the continent, as many drivers stop for biological relief at every opportunity and spread the disease over vast areas.

I guess though it was a hard job to keep track of your jurisdiction when your area stretches in a transverse line for over a 1,000 kilometres. It was home to 168,000 people, with 29 clinics, 4 satellite clinics, 3 community health centres, 8 hospitals, 80 schools on a feeding programme, and you only had 64 staff to deal with it all.

We visited one out-of-town clinic, this time deep, deep rural. It had taken us three hours on a gravel road to reach it. Here we were first introduced to the local policeman.

Our hosts insisted we took shots of his visit where he sat down for a coffee with the matron while they had a long chat. I couldn't understand why he was on the scene, I saw no relevance in him being there at all, and put it down to local courtesy. But no, he was a regular visitor first thing every Monday morning to take the list of names of all those patients who'd come for treatment over the weekend. He would then jump into his patrol car and race off to frighten the life out of all the men who had beaten up their wives, to the extent they in turn were forced to seek treatment at the clinic. Whether this local justice worked over time I have no idea, but quite how to show such flagrant law breaking, committed by an officer who was there to uphold justice, we didn't spell out too clearly.

To be honest, apart from domestic abuse, usually caused by drink at the weekend after they had been paid, or the travelling bank caravan had been, the rest of the community was quiet, peaceful and very welcoming. If you were looking for a place to retire, I think you could live here peacefully, totally unaware of the outside world and all its problems.

The final shot of this programme was a grand old man who told us in Afrikaans that he had no teeth, but he was a 101 years old. Well past wife-beating days I reckoned.

10   ANIMALS & THE DEVIL'S CLAW

It was not only sick people we were asked to film, the animals were not forgotten and we spent days with several veterinary departments as well. As we walked into one surgery in the Northern Cape, we found one of the two veterinarians treating a pile of really cute new-born puppies.

He looked up in horror as we began to roll the cameras. "You can't show this!" he exclaimed. "We are not supposed to treat household pets." Then he paused. "No, turn the camera back on," he instructed, "our job is to educate people about their domestic animals as well, and I turn no one away."

I think they were among the friendliest and kindest people we met, and I still have the porcupine quills they gave us when we eventually waved goodbye.

I was a bit shocked at the farm they took us to, as we stumbled along a muddy track, doing our best to avoid the rusting bicycles, wrecked cars, broken glass and abandoned building materials, to gaze at a pen of depressed and bedraggled chickens which all looked as if they needed a good dose of Prozac.

Nor was I too keen on my first visit to an abattoir to show us the clean, healthy meat facilities the health department boasted about. We walked past a pen of panicking cows being herded towards the stun gun, and then we were shown into a door at the far end. We were handed white coats, un-fetching paper caps and white wellingtons. This first part was not too bad, watching the meat being packed into boxes, ready to be stored into huge refrigerated rooms. But as we walked towards the killing area, ducking the raw meat swaying backwards and forwards on the hooks, I began to get frantic.

The moment I saw the newly killed carcasses still twitching I'd had enough. And clutching Aarnav, I begged him to take me outside. Russell looked at me in astonishment, he simply couldn't understand what all the fuss was about. He'd slit plenty of throats in his time so what was the big deal? I think he lost a little respect for me that day. No, he possibly lost a lot of respect. I guess I was just another example of how weak and pathetic people of European origin could be. It wasn't as if I was even a vegetarian, so where did I think my steaks came from? Was I stupid enough to believe that they materialised out of nowhere onto the little plastic trays in the supermarket?

The only abattoir I coped with was the chicken one, as the conveyor belt was so quick, and in no time at all, they were de-feathered and prepared for the shops. That was until I went outside and saw a local meat seller sitting on the ground, plastic sheet spread out, selling the most indescribable mangled flesh. I could never, ever bring myself to eat any of it.

Are you convinced by now that the media world is not as glamorous as you thought?

Another veterinary department picked us up from our lodgings at 3am and drove us way out of town to show us how they inoculated wild buffalo against TB. I kept well back behind the fence while the ranger took aim and shot them all with his tranquiliser gun.

Next they all had bandages tied around their eyes to lessen the stress, and then needles the size of javelins pumped in the serum, by which time I was brave enough to creep inside the enclosure, but I soon scooted out again when the semi-comatose animals were given their wake-up antidote. I was so impressed with the idea of the blindfolds that was really thoughtful.

Another charming team took us north to the Orange River. As we looked across the water, we could see Namibia on the other side. The finalists proudly showed us the irrigation channels they had dug to water the lucerne they were growing for their new sheep.

"It's never been done before," they told us proudly. I thought of ancient Egypt and nodded, hoping I looked suitably impressed. I was just in time to kick Russell who I could see was just dying to enlighten them about irrigation methods going back centuries. Why spoil their triumph?

We went further inland to see another irrigation scheme using wind pumps, which would encourage sheep farming in the area. These farms were, once again, miles and miles from anywhere, and had been chosen as part of a livestock improvement scheme. I was a bit alarmed when I saw how they casually picked up the unfortunate sheep by their back legs and swung them from one pen to the other, but I assumed they knew what they were doing. I suggested that we not show that on camera though. These were specially bred sheep of enormous value and such rough behaviour did not convey that message too well.

At another veterinary clinic, we were introduced to one of the local farmers who arrived just after us with a huge ram tied up in the back of his pick-up truck, or bakkie as it is called in South Africa.

Great, I thought as I watched him approach. A real live customer, we will get an endorsement from him, which always carries more weight than the views voiced by the contestants themselves.

"And what is the problem?" I asked him with an encouraging smile. I thought this would make a really good interview.

He looked at me as he manhandled the wretched animal off the vehicle. "This 'ere ram is no bloody good," he said. "He won't f**k my sheep."

"Ah, yes, so could you tell us that on camera and then we can show how the staff are going to help you?" He was quite happy to do so. We clipped a radio microphone to his jacket and were ready to roll. "In your own time," I said with an encouraging smile.

"I brought my ram to the clinic 'ere as what he won't f**k my sheep."

"That's great," I said brightly, "but could you say that again for us and uh, not mention the 'f' word? Maybe you could say 'he won't mate with my sheep?'" The farmer nodded and we went to the next take.

"This 'ere ram won't f**k my sheep, bloody queer 'e is."

"Uh, no, that was... well can we leave out the 'f**k' *and* the 'bloody' this time?" He nodded again.

"My ram aint no good, 'e won't f**k my sheep, 'es sodding rubbish."

It was getting steadily worse. I could just imagine the reaction at the awards banquet if I used this version of the interview. I didn't know whether to laugh, or cry, knowing we were spending precious time trying to get a few simple words which would really enhance the insert.

"Take 42.... No, cut!"

We tried again and again and again until at last I thought I would give it one last try. "Do you usually speak Afrikaans?"

"Yes."

"Then maybe you can say it in Afrikaans for us, without the 'f' word? It's not a word we can use in our video." He was quite happy to cooperate.

"Ek het hom hier gebring want die bliksems se ram wil nie my skaap fok nie. Hy is n moffie," said our farmer with a big smile on his face.

I turned to Aarnav, as an Indian he was the only member of the crew who understood Afrikaans, Russell and I only had a handful of words between us.

He sighed and said "I brought him here because this 'ere sodding ram won't f**k my sheep. He's a bloody queer!" At that point I gave up and decided to use a voice-over instead.

To our amazement the staff laid the unfortunate animal out on a board, attached wires to his less-than-private parts, and turned a small wheel that was part of what looked like a tiny hand operated generator.

"What are they doing to it?" I gasped.

"Giving it an orgasm, so we can test the sperm," said the vet next to me. Of course! How stupid of me not to realise that. And I had to ask, didn't I?

A few minutes later I looked down the microscope to see hundreds of wriggling sheep sperm swarming all over the slide. This ram had plenty of testosterone or whatever sheep have.

"Looks as if it might be a homosexual ram," commented the vet.

I gasped at him in amazement. "You get homosexual animals!"

"Oh yes, more often than you'd imagine."

I watched as they all but pronounced the death sentence on the poor creature when the furious farmer drove off in a swirl of dust on his way straight to the slaughter house. I consoled myself that it might die with a smile on its face, having just had a nice experience.

There was one veterinary department which did not impress me, firstly because, as we were travelling in their vehicle to a far-flung farm, we ran over something in the road. I thought they would immediately stop, as the poor creature was screaming in pain behind us, but the vet said there simply wasn't enough time. I still think he could have spared a moment to put the animal out of its misery. I went 'off him' rapidly as they say.

We were on our way to a farm to watch how they killed wild buck, and then have the carcasses inspected by the vet department before being immediately loaded into a refrigerated truck. This was now necessary to meet European Union regulations for imported game, and other Health and Safety factors to ensure the meat was completely disease free. These were wild animals after all and you didn't know where they had been or what they had been up to.

I wasn't aware of all this, it was dark by the time we arrived, and I was not quite sure what to expect. I was puzzled to see a huge refrigerated truck parked in the veld while three men were erecting a steel frame next to it.

I didn't have time to get a good look before I was bundled into the front seat of a bakkie, while Russell and Aarnav stood up in the back with the camera and microphone.

"Here, hold this," said the driver getting in beside me. 'This' was a huge, great gun or a hunting rifle or something like that. I balanced it gingerly on my knees, terrified I might set it off.

I have very little experience with guns, though I had been offered the odd AK47 now and again in the townships.

"Gun very cheap, but bullets expensive," my hopeful vendor had told me as he tried to drag me behind a mud hut. I graciously declined to buy it, it would never fit in the glove compartment and that's where I had seen all those armed people in films from America keep theirs.

But this gun I was holding now was also long, and heavy, and I had no idea if it was loaded. I was tempted to ask, but as the only female around, I felt I had to show I was up to this. Yes, I could be as tough as these hunters. In my dreams.

That night I learned you should never go shooting animals, with or without a gun, under a full moon. It increased the animals' vision and they could run away more easily. But of course as we were there to shoot with the camera, our hosts would fit in with our schedule. Now that was something I had never planned for when setting up the appointment!

I felt quite miserable as we drove over the rough ground. There was no seat belt. My head was banging on the roof and I was terrified the gun would blow me to bits. Every time we caught sight of the buck, the only static ones were the kudu and they were not on the menu. The merciless hunter sitting beside me was after springbok.

"Never mind" I said at last, with my head pounding, and my bum totally numb. "Farmers nil, springboks three!" I thought this was quite witty, as the South African national rugby team is called the Springboks. It was also my suggestion to call it a night.

The farmer gave me a withering look and put his foot on the accelerator, only to slam on the brakes a minute later. Grabbing the gun off my lap he thrust it out of the window and took aim. Bang, bang, bang. Three deer hit the deck. My heart sank, they had not even planned to go shooting, but had set up the whole scenario just for us. Once again, I was indirectly responsible for more animals going to the big game park in the sky, possibly to join the rat I'd condemned a few years earlier.

The carcasses were collected, hung on a convenient post then picked up and taken to the steel frames. Here, they were strung up and split open, while the vets did a thorough examination before stamping them and slinging them into the refrigerated truck. That was another insert in the can.

If I thought the abattoir took some stamina that was before I went to the chicken farms. Yes, in theory they were free range chickens, housed in a barn, and yes, in theory they could run around, if they could find the space to move. I'd thought that *free range* meant running wildly and happily around in a field. But no, as long as they were not in cages they were classified as '*free*'.

The smell was quite indescribable, but the cheerful band of friendly women who greeted us with songs and dances, holding palm fronds in one hand and a chicken dangling upside down in the other, were oblivious to the stench.

When they wanted to move the chickens from one barn to another they waded in amongst them, grabbing legs and bundling half a dozen in each hand, with more squeezed under each armpit, before flinging them over the wall into the next pen. I guessed they knew what they were doing, as after stumbling for a few moments, it looked as if the chickens could still walk.

After we had gathered all the footage we needed at the farm they told us we were going to drive them to a nearby school just down the road, so they could present a few chickens to the children as a public relations exercise. They didn't use those exact words of course, but I could see that their gifts would help keep everyone happy.

I really didn't want a crowd of squawking, screeching chickens in the back of my car, especially as I had no idea how far this school was. In Africa, 'just down the road' could be just that or a hundred kilometres or more. I didn't feel I could refuse to give them a lift in the crew car, which happened to belong to my husband. I borrowed it from him for shoots as it was large, powerful and had an enormous boot.

As one of the ladies came to wait by the car, three

chickens dangling upside down from each hand, I noticed with horror that there were little mite-type creatures leaping about in the chicken feathers. I shuddered. How many would drop off and snuggle down for a sight-seeing drive to visit the rest of the province's finalists? Did these little black creatures bite? Did they carry diseases? And then it also dawned on me that chickens weren't house trained either, though I wasn't sure if they could commune with nature while hanging upside down.

At the last possible moment, much to my relief, another customer arrived in his bakkie to buy chickens, and I managed to persuade him to give the ladies, and their infested birds, a lift to the local school. I bribed him with the promise he would be on national television, and I would get the finalists to say on camera how delicious these particular chickens were, and how he was their favourite customer. I lifted my eyes to heaven and hoped that He would forgive my lies. It was all in a good cause wasn't it? I was only protecting the health of my crew.

And these chicken ladies were also tough I observed, as they posed on the verandah with the happy, smiling schoolchildren singing their thanks for the presents. They casually picked up the birds, calmly wrung their necks then began to pluck the feathers out of the warm squirming bodies.

This was just one more example of what could be achieved by working together and how the average African woman was reliable, consistent and worked particularly hard. We saw so many examples of this from road building to gardening, house construction and vegetable growing. In one instance we were sad to learn that previous attempts to grow maize had failed, because the moment the corn was almost ripe, thieves broke in and stole the lot. The women switched to cotton, which no one ran off with.

A few years later, on another project, this time for an egg company, we were taken to another chicken farm, and this time the poor creatures were all encased five to a small wire cage. They were in a terrible condition, and although our client did not really understand the need, I protested that we just could not shoot them all cramped up like that. It would simply not be good for their public relations image and would put customers off, not attract them.

The programme was to encourage the public to buy eggs in a new kind of container, which was quite space-age and innovative. It announced in bold letters on the side that it contained 'farm fresh eggs, from happy, free range chickens'. Well these birds were not free and they most certainly were not even the slightest bit amused either.

So, could we not get a few of the poor creatures out of their cages and put them out on the grass? I asked. Here I go again with the blatant propaganda, but I knew what the client wanted and once again, who was going to sign the cheque. At the same time, if I could see his marketing campaign was going to go right down the tubes by giving the Hollywood treatment to cages of suffering and confined bedraggled egg layers, then I didn't want the blame for that either. Survival for the one with the bright ideas right?

The farm workers agreed to let the creatures out, even though they did not understand my repulsion and that of the crew, at seeing them treated so badly. A couple of the men went off to collect the chickens and I began pushing and shoving hay bales around to form a barrier so they wouldn't escape.

"What are you doing? Do you want to sit down? We can fetch a chair for you."

"No, no I'm making a barrier so the chickens won't escape. We can put them inside this space here," I replied.

"No, that won't be necessary. They won't run away," they seemed quite sure of this.

"Well just in case," I persisted, "you will promise to catch them yourselves afterwards? You won't need us to help you do that?" The last thing I felt like doing on a boiling hot day was running around like an idiot helping them to catch the chickens. I'd seen too many times in the past how fast those little monsters could run.

"No, no, it's not necessary." They were quite insistent, and I thought they just didn't know much about chickens. OK, I reasoned, if you want to spend the next few hours trying to round up the birds as they bolted for freedom into the next province, be it on your own heads.

But they were right.

When they carried the birds over, and set them on the ground, the chickens stood stock-still, frozen to the spot. They didn't move at all and at first I couldn't understand it. Then it dawned on me, I don't think they knew how to walk, much less run. Maybe I wasn't doing them a favour either by insisting they come out of their tiny prisons. They had gone into a complete state of shock.

Now they were out in broad daylight they looked even more moth eaten and bald than they had indoors. You could clearly see the running sores all over their bodies and the gaps where their feathers were missing. It was really difficult to get camera angles which made the chickens look as if they were not on their last legs and ready for the big chicken run in the sky, followed by the cooking pot.

For over two hours we struggled to make them look like the happy, healthy chickens you saw in the pictures displayed above their eggs in the supermarket. And this was the farm the egg company had taken us to, to show off their egg producers. It was unbelievable.

I didn't eat an egg for a month, nor could I face a piece of chicken.

There were several schemes which were set up to encourage people to stay on the land, and not swarm into the cities and settle in the squatter camps looking for work that was not to be found. Despite all the minerals hidden under the ground, up on the Reef above, the streets in Johannesburg and Pretoria were not paved with gold.

One of these rural projects was a gladioli farm in the far Northern Cape area. If we thought it had been hot before, that day the camera seized up in the heat and gave me a heart attack. It was the last time I would go on location with only one camera.

The flower project was very impressive, rows and rows of gladioli stretched away into the distance, all under shade cloth. I must get a few comments from the cooperative farmers, I thought and approached a likely looking candidate.

"Would you like to tell us what you think of the flower farm?" I asked.

"Humph," was the reply. "They wouldn't let us grow mealies and potatoes, that's what we want to grow. Not stupid flowers."

"Uh, right, well, yes, uh, thank you very much," and I went in search of someone a little more enthusiastic.

"Are you part of this consortium growing the flowers?" I asked another smiling lady.

Her smile disappeared rapidly. "Yes, but only because the chief told me I had to work here. I wanted to grow food for my family, but all these," she indicated the rows and rows of flowers, "all these are sent away to be sold."

"But surely you earn money by looking after the flowers, and use that to buy food?" I asked.

"It's easier to grow my own vegetables, it is cheaper, and I don't have to walk a long way to the shops," was the reply.

She did have a point. Once again, this farm was in the middle of nowhere, and as far as the eye could see, there was not another building in sight. When I asked about this, all I got was an airy wave of the hand indicating that they all lived in *that* direction.

I tried to interview six more people, but they all had the same story, and not one of them was happy about the project.

I would love to have found out why the flower farm was in this precise location, who was really benefitting from it, and who had taken the unpopular decision to set up the project in the first place. Was this a community working together? Or a few people at the top making money for themselves on the back of a government grant?

But our job was not investigative documentary making, although that would have been my dream. No, our job was to make these people look good and show how it was all working.

As soon as we began to interview the leaders of the scheme we got many enthusiastic replies, and those were the only ones I included in the final video.

I went even further and persuaded one of the project management team to 'pretend' to be a farmer who was delighted by the floral growth! Yes I know this borders on propaganda, well on out-and-out lies really, but you don't believe everything you see on the TV do you? We were there to capture what we were told to record.

Not all agricultural projects were a disaster, some were working well. We were taken to a bulb farm which, from a distance, looked just like acres and acres of bare earth, but as we got closer, we saw miniature figures bent over, beavering away in long rows, patiently planting, or digging. It looked back-breaking work and I was glad I didn't have to do it. I was even more thankful when it was time to get out of the blazing heat and take shelter in the huge shed which housed the bulbs as they were packed for export.

There was definitely a different mindset among this group, for as we were leaving, they loaded up the car with several boxes of bulbs. It wasn't the first time we had been given small gifts, as I've mentioned, we'd received grapes and porcupine quills and painted rocks in the past, and we thought this was just another token of appreciation and another demonstration of African hospitality and sharing.

We were wrong. Next they presented us with the bill, and it was not for a small amount either. We could hardly refuse. I could see this entrepreneurial group knew the meaning of true capitalism and salesmanship!

For a brief moment, as I forked out the money from my small operating budget to pay for the bulbs, I hoped they would last to the end of the shoot and we were all back at home. I considered asking the rest of the crew if they would like bulbs on toast for supper that night, but decided that would not be received too favourably. I would have to bite the bullet and visit the nearest ATM on the way back to the bed and breakfast.

I was concerned about one food production project when I realised that our subject specialist, who was the Provincial Minister for Agriculture herself, was unaware the whole scheme was using a variety of GM (genetically modified) maize. While the crops grew big and healthy, it meant the farmers had to buy new seeds each year, which kept them locked-in to the suppliers. In the long term this may not be the answer to Africa's food production, it sacrifices their freedom to grow and produce independently.

I was very curious about one finalist's name that was entitled simply 'Devil's Claw', along with the address and the telephone number of the manager in charge. As the years went on, that often became the sum total of the information we were given before we set off to make a five minute video about them.

We were trusted as experts on the different principles of service, openness, transparency, courtesy, giving best value, access, standards, and so on and I began to think we could do this in our sleep.

But 'Devil's Claw'? It couldn't be a school, or a housing scheme or a library, or road maintenance, not with a name like that surely? For once we did not know what to expect, we hadn't the faintest idea what it was all about.

I phoned the manager and he said he would send one of his team to the guest house at seven the following morning. I sighed, another session of quick talking to the guest house owners to provide an extra early breakfast. In South Africa most people are early risers, but breakfast as early as 6.15am was asking rather a lot.

It was just as well the manager sent us a guide as we would never have found the distant rural location. We were directed to pull up outside what looked like a village hall which towered over a few scattered huts and small agricultural plots showing a row of wilted cabbages and other green leafy things I couldn't identify.

As we got out of the car, the leader rushed up to greet us, smiling and shaking hands all round. He assured me that they were all ready for us, and a long line of notable local bigwigs stood in line ready for more handshaking.

We were then instructed to off-load the gear and follow them into the hall, and I was handed a piece of paper, carefully typed, with the heading

ORDER OF THE DAY

REASON FOR DAY – MRS LUCINDA CLARKE.

This was followed by a long list of events and the times they were starting and finishing.

I gasped! *'I'* was the reason for the day? *Me*? I looked further down the list. We would start with prayers, followed by a meeting with the local community led by the chief, and after that I was to be introduced, and then give a speech. They expected me to stand up front and talk? Didn't they understand the whole concept of these awards? The team and I were here just to record *their* achievements, not to make a fuss of *our* visit! I was not looking forward to making any kind of speech, what did they expect me to say?

I quaked as they ushered us into the hall where there were rows and rows of benches all occupied by the entire population of the area, all dressed in their best clothes. The crew were looking our usual scruffy selves in crew T-shirts and jeans.

At that point in my life, apart from teaching, lecturing, and the odd boardroom discussions, I'd little experience of talking to groups of people, especially without any warning at all. There was also the small problem that I had no idea what these people did, what they had achieved, and what I was supposed to say to them.

I gracefully tried to tell them that this was not really necessary, I was here to find out what *they* did, I was not important at all, but they were having none of it.

No, they insisted, it was not every day they had important people from the television to visit and they had also prepared a huge lunch for us.

I groaned, another group who thought we were here from the SABC, and I just hoped they would not sit for hours in front of their televisions waiting to see themselves on the small screen.

We all began with a prayer, a common custom in Africa, each day would often start with a hymn. Time and time again I was caught out, in the middle of muddy fields, in boardrooms and offices and staff rooms and classrooms and hospital rest rooms. Every day, every event and every occasion began with a prayer. Those early missionaries must have been really busy and I remember reading that at one time, in Natal especially, there were more religious orders per square kilometre than anywhere else on earth.

As the last 'Amen' died away, I was announced. Reluctantly I got to my feet and I can't remember what I said, but I spoke generally about the awards themselves, stuff they all knew about anyway, and how we were going to show all the 'good practices they had been practising,' (they knew that as well of course) and how I hoped everyone was going to enjoy the experience.

There followed more long speeches from the local chief of course and other important people and I was grateful they had picked us up so early.

However, the day turned out to be a great success. We discovered that the Devil's Claw is a plant that grows in the area. No one had taken much notice of it, although the *sangomas* or witchdoctors had used it to cure all kinds of complaints for years. Then it came to the notice of the pharmaceutical and natural healing companies in Europe, and after extensive testing (which showed its potential in relieving the pain caused by arthritis) the race was on to get their hands on it.

The Africans use it to cure pain, for difficulties in childbirth, loss of appetite, gastric problems and heart burn, fever and headaches. They also apply it to the skin for injuries and skin complaints.

The local people here were really switched on. They

recognised the benefits this could bring for everyone and, in an agreement with representatives from Germany, they undertook to harvest and sell the plant. No wonder the audience was so smartly dressed, this was obviously a very profitable cash crop.

When they took us out to the area where they were currently harvesting I was puzzled. I couldn't see any plants anywhere, the bare, dusty earth was devoid of any crops and the top soil was completely undisturbed. So where was this plant, or whatever it was? The Devil's Claw is a tuber, rather like a wizened potato, but with hook-like protuberances.

We were shown how the men and women dug down and uncovered the root, carefully cut off the sharp bits which they put to one side, and then re-buried the rest of it back in the soil. They were clever enough to harvest in a sustainable manner, so they would never run out of product as the tubers regenerated again.

The one thing that did puzzle me was how they knew where to dig. One elderly lady, who had changed out of her finery, stared at a bare piece of earth, and then pounced and began scrabbling at the soil. Sure enough, a few inches down, she uncovered a root.

I asked her how she knew the tuber was in that exact spot, but she shrugged her shoulders and smiled. She just 'knew'.

This delightful group of people had also rehearsed and put on a small play for us. The cast included a patient, a witch doctor and a family member who brought the ailing youth to be cured. It was so well done and, thankfully, it did not go on for hours and hours. It was a great day's shoot and one of the most colourful as well. Even the lunch included a fresh, appetising salad I felt was safe to eat, leaving the rest of the crew to take their chances with the bits of unnamed flesh floating in its usual watery sauce.

In all it was a really enjoyable day, as most of our agricultural visits were. One vet department took us to a cattle dip out in the middle of nowhere where I remember my favourite shot. A smiling boy about ten years old, holding a frayed bit of string which was attached to an old leather collar round the neck of his dog. He'd walked over 12 kilometres that morning after he heard the vets were coming, as he had learned that they could put needles in his dog so he wouldn't get sick. Yes, some mindsets in Africa were changing.

We travelled to Gauteng, (the new name for the Transvaal), which promised to be very exciting as one of the projects was described as a new game reserve. It was always a thrill to get close to the wildlife, as each year there are fewer and fewer animals due to the heartbreaking and relentless poaching.

We picked up our guide and followed his directions out of town. As we sped further north I noticed the sign that said we were now leaving Gauteng and entering the North West Province. Tentatively I mentioned this to our guide who quite cheerfully told me that yes, it was just a little outside, but as the paperwork was being handled in Johannesburg, they were including this as well, so it really wasn't that important. How that fitted into the awards criteria for each province I was not sure, but then ours was not to reason why. By now I had learned to take it all in my stride and told Russell to roll the camera.

In fact many of the finalists we shot in the main cities in Gauteng were a big disappointment. Most of them did not show great service to the community or improvements for the people. They were showcase projects, such as the new Nelson Mandela Bridge, the paving of a new open space with little statues on either side and other major building works.

For most of these we had to shoot the models in little glass cases, and record meetings, both indoors and outdoors. To fill in extra time, I was even desperate enough to show the main players walking in and out of their offices, and I made them walk in very slowly and kept the camera rolling until they were seated behind their desks, real scintillating stuff I'm sure you will agree. I shamelessly stretched it even further by directing them to walk quickly into a meeting room and take their places at the conference table, breaking up the shot with cutaways of the papers they were carrying. I guess you have a good idea of how desperate I was.

Yes, it sounds pretty pathetic, but I had a time slot to fill and the video for each finalist had to be exactly the same length. When I was struggling to find anything interesting to film I would attempt to make it more exciting in edit, by ghosting plans and drawings over the top.

Another thing I remembered about the shoot in Gauteng (we only ever shot the awards there once), was the number of high-up, important people who pitched up, quite by chance, at the same time and place as we were shooting. Since most government and political people lived in the cities on the Reef they would know what we had been asked to record. So, ministers would just happen to visit a project, pop their head round the door during a meeting, or slide into a desk in a classroom and smile brightly for the camera.

In edit, I ruthlessly cut most of them out, it was the only chance I got to play God, since it was so obvious they were going for brownie points after contributing little or nothing to the success of the various projects. They were just grandstanding and making mileage from the work done by those minions who had really put in the time, effort and enthusiasm. Although the people on the ground involved in the upliftment efforts knew who the ministers were, it was blatantly apparent that the ministers and officials themselves hadn't a clue what was going on. I gave them the axe when I could.

The most outstanding area we went to was once again in the Northern Cape, called the Richtersveld, a large area bordering the Kalahari Desert. It was way off the beaten track, and the directions we had for getting there were vague to say the least. We would be heading out there into the wilderness, miles from anywhere and I didn't fancy getting lost, possibly with no reliable maps and no cell phone coverage.

I decided to dent the budget and hire a four wheel drive vehicle complete with driver, and we set off at 4am, as it was going to take several hours to get there from our base in the town of Springbok.

The landscape took our breath away, low rolling hills, no trees and thousands and thousands of small, succulent plants nestling close to the ground. The whole community was up for the award, for their efforts to attract tourism, and to this end they had furnished two small guest houses way outside their small village. The land was communally owned and they had set up a small tourist office on the main gravelled high street, which comprised of a community centre and one lonely shop.

This was one of the few occasions we met a whole community of the real descendants of the original peoples of southern Africa, the San and the Khoekhoe peoples (often referred to as Bushmen). They are much shorter than the black Bantus, and all of them have wizened, yellowish complexions and bright twinkly eyes. Their huts are built solely of grass, and many of them still wandered from place to place according to the seasons. Their customs and their culture are also different, and they appeared to live in complete harmony with nature.

One of the elders took us for a walk, and showed us how you could survive solely from the liquid found in so many plants, and he pointed out those which were safe to eat and which ones to avoid. It was such an amazing experience that it was very difficult to tear ourselves away, back to civilisation, although Springbok was hardly in the mainstream of the modern world. I used some of the things he told me in my novel about 'Amie'. He had proved to me that you can survive even in the most inhospitable places.

Later that night back in Springbok in their one and only Italian restaurant (it was my turn to choose), the waiter said he had never heard of the 'Parmesan cheese' I wanted on my spaghetti bolognese. He even went to ask the chef if he knew about this 'Parmesan cheese' stuff, and he came out of the kitchen looking quite perplexed. No, he'd never heard of it either. I decided not to tell him that it had been around since the thirteenth century and this was the first time I had eaten Italian food without it.

We took a few moments out to explore one particular shop in Springbok. Downstairs it was a dairy, but upstairs, they had a restaurant and a whole range of things for sale, especially the wide variety of semi-precious stones found naturally all over the area, such as rose quartz, tiger's eye, verdite, agate, moss opal, obsidian, onyx, beryl and jasper. These we scooped up by the bagful. They had already been polished and were a fraction of the cost you would pay anywhere else.

This northern part of South Africa is rich in minerals, and vast areas of the Northern Cape are under concession to the big mining companies. Sadly we never had much time to explore, and we couldn't reach the coast due to it being a restricted area, where they mine alluvial diamonds in the shallow waters of the South Atlantic.

While the landscape is harsh and bleak, there is a certain majesty and awe about it. It's a semi-desert and there might be little or no rainfall for months at a time. Everything looks dead with only a low growth of bracken-type vegetation and small cacti. Until the rain falls. Then whole area turns into a mass of flowers, pink and white and yellow and blue, like a huge carpet spread throughout the valleys, which for a few brief weeks, softens the landscape. The Namaqualand daisies are famous and people travel from all over the world to see them.

We had to take care when travelling the vast distances between locations, sometimes as many as 450 kilometres apart, as the tarred roads were flat, straight and stretched as far as the eye could see. After a couple of hours, it could become a blur, and it was easy to lose concentration and fall asleep.

There was also the danger of speed. Once to my horror, I discovered that the speedometer was hovering around 180 kilometres an hour. There was nothing to judge your speed by, except for the telegraph and electric poles lining the road on either side. If you passed more than half a dozen other cars on your journey, it was a lot, and I often prayed we would not break down as there was limited cell phone coverage on many stretches.

I remember teasing Russell in a town called Uppington. I took him outside the hotel and told him I wanted a few shots of the main street at rush hour.

He looked at me. "And when is that?" he asked.

"Any time now," I replied.

"But I can't see any cars!" he exclaimed, and then the penny dropped and he laughed and laughed and laughed. Personally I didn't think it was all *that* funny, but apart from no cars, at 5 o'clock in the evening, there wasn't a single pedestrian to be seen either!

11 PROTECT & DESTROY

One department I've not mentioned and frequently nominated as award finalists, were the police, or rather the road traffic units, and perhaps they were the biggest cowboys of all. Year after year they threw themselves into the part and had it all planned out before we could unload the camera equipment.

They set up scenarios which involved road chases, when we would go screaming down the freeways, blue lights flashing, horns blasting, setting up arrests and chasing perpetrators. They sent a 'criminal' up a tree and got the dogs to snarl below, they mocked up road accidents and they threw up speed traps and road blocks and inspected vehicles for us.

Once again we were the catalyst which caused a young student to have her car confiscated on her way to an examination, as it was deemed unsafe, while another brand-new vehicle was hauled away for being illegally imported. Several other motorists were dragged off after being breathalysed at 10 o'clock in the morning. While we assume that we'll be fine the next day after a heavy night's drinking, apparently this is not always the case, it takes longer than you think for alcohol to drain out of the system.

On one occasion they even blocked off the main

freeway from Johannesburg to Durban and pounced on a car which had passed its roadworthy test a week earlier. Just seven days later it was missing a steering wheel (the driver used a wrench on the steering column instead). The passenger door fell off when the police opened it, and there were several holes in the floor. The bumpers were hanging on by a thread and there was more rust than steelwork in the frame. It was the funniest thing we'd seen for ages.

Just as we were shooting a truck on a weighbridge, the driver suddenly screamed and fell to the ground. We rushed to help.

"No, no!" they shouted. "He's supposed to do that, we want to show you how we revive him. We've all had First Aid training." The *patient* got sheepishly to his feet and we started all over again.

In another town they had rehearsed an hour-long play for us to film, and I felt very guilty cutting it short after 10 minutes, explaining that we had to show *everything* they did in 5 minutes. I'm not sure they were convinced. That was in a rural police station which, in the days before motorised transport, had gone out on patrol on the backs of camels! I thought they were joking, until I saw the large statue of a policeman on the back of a camel right outside the police station.

Sometimes it was difficult to keep a straight face. A prime achievement for one group was the development of a portable rubber speed hump that could lie in wait for unsuspecting motorists. Once we were asked to show trucks with the signage spelt all wrong.

I have to admit we burst out laughing the day the cops

were so busy role playing for us they failed to notice (to be honest, we did as well) that a couple of lads had quietly got into the police car parked off to one side and driven it away. We kindly offered a couple of them a ride back to the police station.

There was also the case of the disgraced team, but I'll come to them in a minute.

There was the more serious side to the policing though. Many stations had set up trauma rooms for rape victims and a support system for those who suffered domestic abuse. This was a relatively new concept, and I was reminded of an incident a few years earlier when we had been filming a mock-up lesson for our star cop in the '*I Want to Join the Police Force*' film.

One young policeman had been chosen to explain to a class of eager students, the new regulations for what they should do when called out to a compliant about family violence. The young lecturer had not got very far when an elderly African policeman at the back of the room got to his feet.

"What nonsense is this!" he exclaimed loudly. "We are policemen and it is not for us to go and stop a man from beating his wife and children. He has every right to do that, it is not criminal."

"But there have been changes in the law," the flustered lecturer replied.

"Then the law is stupid. A man has the perfect right to chastise his wife if she will not sleep with him, or her cooking is not good, or she displeases him. I will not go out to a case like that!"

I indicated to the crew that we should pack up quietly

and leave the room, feeling rather guilty abandoning the young policeman at the front of the class to talk his way out of that one. Yes, things were changing, but it would take a lot longer for mindsets to catch up, and they move more slowly than we assume.

A really innovative idea from one road traffic department was the completely foolproof driving test they had introduced, featuring the most up to date technology in the world.

A common cry when someone behaved badly on the roads was to shout out of the car window, "Where did you buy your driving licence? Checkers?" (referring to a local supermarket chain).

This wasn't really a joke. It was estimated that there were probably as many people driving on the roads with fake licences as there were drivers who had passed their tests. Add to that the number of those who didn't bother with any kind of paperwork at all, and you may get the idea that driving could be just a little dangerous.

At one testing station where we filmed they offered me a licence for my daughter, after I had mentioned she was about to take her test for the second time and the lessons were costing me a fortune. For a brief millisecond I was tempted, but then I could never be party to sending anyone out on the roads in charge of a potentially lethal weapon without the skill to control it.

Now, I'm not sure that in the meantime test centres around the world have not introduced these following foolproof measures, but I couldn't see how you could possibly cheat. When you booked the appointment to take the written test, the staff took a retina scan. Apparently your eye print is unique to you much like fingerprints and obviously impossible to fake. I guess you can eradicate your fingertips with acid, but I wouldn't like to try that on my eyes.

The written test was then carefully monitored, and as it was all computerised, tricky to cheat. When it came to the actual car driving bit, the candidate was primed in a room with the examiner while CCTV recorded every word. Basic driving on the in-station course was also visually taped and it was mandatory to use one of the twelve specially equipped cars provided at the test centre. These were also fitted with audio and visual recording devices and even when out on the road test, all the information from the in-car cameras and microphones was stored on a hard drive located in the boot. The moment the car drove back in through the gates, the recording was downloaded via an electronic eye, and instantly sent on its way to Johannesburg, and a pass or fail recorded.

I have no idea if anyone has cracked this security by now, but it took combined technology from Britain, Canada and South Africa to put it all together and make it as foolproof as possible. I was amazed and so was Carl, to the extent that he quite forgot to roll the camera!

Back to the disgraced team I mentioned earlier. It was another road traffic department and we had originally planned to shoot them on a Friday, but I had to reschedule as another finalist had a problem, so I swapped them and we went in to record them on the Thursday. As usual, they put on a really good show, and we were all over the place, arresting 'criminals', resuscitating 'heart attacks' and chasing 'runaways' down the freeway. At lunch time they treated us to an amazing lunch and as we drove home I was thinking what a nice bunch of guys they were.

On Saturday morning I opened the local newspaper, no I didn't even have to open it, because there, on the front page, was the news that the whole team had been busted on the Friday and all the office computers confiscated for being crammed full of kiddie porn.

In shock, I rang one of the project managers and told him. "What do we do?" I asked. "They are finalists in this year's awards, and now they are possibly in jail! How can they be a shining light in good service delivery?"

"Goodness, how terrible!" he replied. "I'll get back to you."

So what happened? Regarding the prosecutions, I have no idea, but I can tell you that they stayed in the finals and won an award. I felt it rather devalued everything we were trying to show, and I ground my teeth in fury as they bounced up onto the stage, grinning from ear to ear, to meet the premier and collect their trophy. Ah well, you live and learn.

Another disastrous project I remember vividly started off as a great idea but totally backfired, not of course that we were able to show the truth of this. It was common knowledge that children had to walk many miles each day to and from school. Older children often dropped out if they could find work closer to home, or got bored with school. This scheme offered them a bicycle on long term loan, so they could stay on to complete their education.

I was feeling very enthusiastic as we drove up to the

school at 7am to film the children riding into school. By the time the gates were firmly shut an hour later, not one bicycle had arrived.

We traipsed into the playground and the headmaster sent us off with one of the teachers to find the bikes. It took a bit of searching, but at last he tracked down two abandoned bicycles in a store room. Both of them had flat tyres and the back wheel of one curved delicately at right angles to the frame.

I gazed at the wrecks in horror. What were we going to do?

"And the reflective arm bands, and the helmets?" I asked quietly.

"Oh, they are here somewhere."

Yes, they were. One of them was cracked and the other had a large dent at the back. The remaining three arm bands had provided an excellent breeding nest for moths, and they didn't sparkle or reflect any more.

It took us hours and hours to shoot. First two children on the bikes, then another two, then a third pair, same bicycles, different children, in the hope it would look as if all original 24 bicycles were still in use. Only we couldn't really show the bicycles properly, as neither was even faintly roadworthy.

To make matters even more difficult, it was impossible to find any children who could ride a bicycle and I wondered how those who were presented with them, in the first place, had coped.

I was trying not to panic and Aarnav only just stopped me in time from assaulting passing cyclists, using the dedicated cycle path outside the school, and hijacking *their* bicycles. We shot every inch of the cycle lane as well, including the cycle sign.

"Maybe an interview," I suggested. "We could use up another 20 seconds that way. Can we talk to one of the boys who was given a bicycle?" I asked the staff. Blank looks all round.

"No."

"Are they not at school?"

"No, they are not here today."

"None of them?"

"No."

"Well we are in the area for the next few days, maybe we could pop in on Friday morning, early? Will they be here then?"

"Maybe not."

"When did you last see these boys?"

"The day after they got their bikes."

So it seemed the moment the new bicycles were handed out, the new owners simply disappeared with them.

By now I was really trying not to panic. Once again I had been commissioned to show something that was not there to show.

"How about some road safety lessons or filming the children looking after the bicycles?" (Although frankly it was a bit late for that). But my suggestions were met with blank stares. Rather reluctantly they set up a classroom and the teacher stood at the front by the blackboard and looked at me with confusion written all over her face.

"Road safety?" she asked, just above a whisper.

"Yes, you know, the rules when you are out and about on the roads," I replied helpfully.

She shrugged and looked totally lost.

In record time I had scribbled down a few pointers. We drove on the left, stopped at traffic lights and pedestrian crossings, and the importance of the solid and broken, white lines painted on the roads.

Even before she began this impromptu lesson she looked less than enthusiastic and as she was speaking, I decided to use a voice-over to cover her lacklustre performance. I could at least encourage the actress we would use in a few weeks time, to add some excitement to the proceedings.

I then resorted to interviews with the management team in town and still photographs of the presentation ceremony when the new bicycles were given to the pupils with, of course, lots of pictures of the brand new cycle track.

Over the 9 years we worked on the 'People First' scheme, I calculated that we shot over 150 different inserts, each a 5 minute programme. The more people we met and the more we were shown, the more I realised how little I knew.

Take the 'places of safety' we were sent to film. I assumed that these were set up to protect children from their parents, or local gangs, or other situations where they had suffered abuse. These were sanctuaries where they could be safe and protected and no one could hurt them. I was only partially right.

I was not unduly surprised to see the first one we visited was securely fenced in, with a guard on the gate. Many schools and government offices and even agricultural projects were surrounded by fences and razor wire. Crime is a big problem.

Inside the facility we were shown the woodwork shop, the educational classes, the sewing room, and all the other activities the children had access to.

There was one particular girl who seemed to take a liking to me and she followed me round the whole day, asking questions and telling me what she'd been doing. I warmed to this gentle, friendly girl. She must have been 13 or 14 years old.

It took me a little while to understand that a place of safety was not there to protect the children from society, but to protect society from the children. They were all incarcerated, either awaiting trial or waiting to be sentenced. Each of them had committed a really serious offence.

I know I should never have asked, but I couldn't resist the temptation and mentioned my new 'friend' to the supervisor.

"She murdered her father and then butchered him into small chunks," he replied. "Of course I shouldn't be telling you this, but I could see she stayed close to you all day."

I stopped in my tracks. That sweet, cheerful, talkative, lovable girl had actually taken a life? She had killed her father? Of course there was no way I could enquire about the circumstances or the causes of her crime, so I never found out, but it gave me such a shock. Then I rationalised, and began to make up all kinds of stories. Maybe her father had been abusing her or the other children, maybe he'd been an aggressive drunk, maybe... well anything, anything rather than think of this sweet faced, innocent looking, young girl as a cold blooded murderer. I often wonder what happened to her.

The other place of safety we visited was for younger children and they only remained there for up to 6 months.

"Just as we have begun to bond with them, they are moved on," one social worker told me sadly. "They still go to school each day and we take them on outings as often as funds allow. But although we work hard with them, they are either sent to a children's home, or returned to their families, often back into the same corrosive atmosphere that caused their problems in the first place."

It was another reminder that families could be a two edged sword.

There was one thing that both places had in common. Almost all the children were HIV positive.

One finalist organisation that really impressed me was a large drug rehabilitation centre run by an amazing team with unlimited passion for their work. They had befriended an AIDS orphanage and inmates from the centre were heavily involved in its upkeep, and fostered the little children whose life expectancy was severely limited. It was a situation that made the in-patients think very deeply about their own issues with dependency.

The centre accepted people from all walks of life, and there was a particularly touching moment when, in their daily assembly, they gave out cards to anyone with a birthday. A young African was called up and presented with his card. I'm not sure if he could read it or not, but he had never received a birthday card before, they had to explain what it was. It was a kind gesture and it reduced him to tears.

One thing I did notice was that all the staff and most of the patients too, smoked like chimneys.

We also visited many housing departments as there was a crying need for more accommodation in a country where the birth rate was high and climbing, and the infant mortality rate was low and falling.

The national government had a scheme to build thousands and thousands of low-cost houses, and at one time it bore the impressive title of the 'Reconstruction and Development Plan'.

The result was row upon row of small, square, breeze block houses with two or at most three, rooms topped with a tin roof. Much of the construction was farmed out to local people, often with little or no training in building work of any kind. But there were targets to be met and not enough qualified builders to go around, so untrained people were employed as managers and quality controllers.

I asked on one occasion why they were erecting houses like this. The traditional African house is made of mud and dung walls topped by a thatched roof, keeping it warm in winter and cool in summer. Visitors who'd stayed with us from overseas had expressed their dismay on seeing these tasteless and inappropriate homes huddled together marching over the hillsides.

"The modern Africans don't want a round house," I was told. "They aspire to a square house, and many have forgotten the traditional skills used in building homes for themselves."

I briefly remembered our *'How to Build a Better*

Squatter House' programme. We had shown them how. I had already experienced how hot these tacky houses were in summer under a metal roof that radiated the heat, and how quickly they let the heat out in winter. Tin roofs provided no insulation at all.

On only one occasion we saw more traditional building, using hardened mud and clay blocks. While I was pleased to see this, I was not so pleased to see they were still using donkeys to work the water into the dry earth. These poor beasts were walking mindlessly round and round in circles in the mid-day heat, and when I asked if they had access to water, my question was met with blank stares.

Sometimes these new township houses had an internal water supply, sometimes there was a tap out in the street. A few had toilets indoors, although one happy homeowner we interviewed told us cheerfully that she had been waiting over a year for the builders to put a door on the smallest room. I hoped that I would not need to use her loo while we were there!

A few contractors, mostly women as they were the most reliable, told us they had been fired from certain tasks as their work had not been up to standard, but that was all right, as now they were responsible for another part of the building procedure instead. Words failed me and in fact we saw some really awful examples of bad workmanship and I wondered just how long it would be before some of these houses came tumbling down.

We were careful not to stand outside the walls under the makeshift scaffolding or inside the walls under a partially completed roof, as many of the building practices were positively dangerous. The breeze blocks powdered against your clothes if you rubbed along a wall, and we had to cover the equipment to prevent the dust getting inside the camera and the microphones.

The smartest housing we saw had been built by some Scandinavians, as an experiment in eco-friendly construction. With their solar panels (which had been mandatory on all new houses in Botswana for over 20 years) together with innovative insulation techniques, rain catching gutters and several other features, running costs had been slashed to a minimum.

Perhaps the saddest housing project we went to was an area 30 kilometres north of a provincial capital, and some background information is necessary to explain how it all came about.

There was a scheme throughout South Africa at the time to award sums of money as reparation for confiscated land. In this case, by putting all the grant money together in trust, a 17,000 hectare farm called Platfontein became the new home for about 7,000 San people of the KhoiSan, the !Xu and the Khwe tribes. In total there were about 800 families from the different tribes, which was not an ideal situation.

Earlier, between 1987 and 1988 they had been flown, with all their belongings, to a town called Schmitsdrift where they were housed in army tents until the next stage in re-housing them. They were originally from Angola, Botswana and Namibia, and during the border wars they had worked closely with the South African National Defence Force as soldiers and trackers. When the war ended they were offered the opportunity to stay in South Africa. Many accepted since in their home country they were now regarded as traitors. Finally, they had been permanently re-housed on this large farm.

The moment we arrived in this partially built housing project, we could see it was different to the residential settlements we'd filmed before. The homes were spaced further apart, there was a tap at the end of each garden and pairs of chemical toilets some distance away. But still, they were all built from the usual grey, powdery breeze block squares and the ubiquitous tin roofs.

We were shown into a couple of the houses by the project management team. Each one contained the bare minimum, a bed, spears on the wall and a couple of logs which I guessed would be used as seating. There were no spare clothes, no sofas or dining room sets on hire purchase from 'Ellerines' or other furniture stores. There were no cooking facilities, the San cooked outdoors on small fires they lit by their front doors.

We were told that approximately ninety-five per cent of them were unemployed, poverty was rife, and many suffered from post traumatic stress disorder. Alcoholism was also a huge problem and relations with the government and council officials were often difficult.

I watched one elderly wizened man as he honed a hunting spear, and was told that I should not include that in the video, as technically, it was illegal to make weapons in South Africa.

I saw no one smile, and despite the management team trying to mock-up a meeting with the local interpreter, the pervasive atmosphere was one of depression, loss of hope and general misery.

"I understand that these San cannot return to their

ancestral homes," I mentioned to one of our subject specialists, "but they don't seem very happy here."

"They will settle down in time," was the firm reply.

"But we're miles away from Kimberley," I said, "and I don't see any signs of public transport. How will they get to work?"

"It will all take time, but we have helped fast track their applications for identity books, and a school has been opened in the area. We have also coordinated the installation of the urine diversion toilets, and the provision of water and electricity to each of the houses."

Yes, this was all good work, but what of the people? Is this what *they* wanted?

"Did anyone suggest, when the farm was bought, that it could have been stocked with game and the San allowed to live by hunting and gathering and building their own traditional houses?" I asked.

There was a shocked silence. "Goodness, what an idea! They *must* be brought into the 21st century, and offered the chance to lead a regular life."

I remembered seeing programmes on television, where the same thing was happening in Botswana. The San people had been forced off their land and were now unwillingly working as low paid farmhands for local farmers.

I also remembered the little San boy I'd had in my class when I was teaching in Francistown in Botswana all those years ago. The African children refused to play with him, and called him derogatory names, teasing him because his skin was yellow and not black.

Slowly but surely these proud people, with their vast

knowledge of living in harmony with nature, were being wiped out through integration and enforced new world values. Their plight was possibly worse than that of those Bantu Africans who had fought so hard for their freedom from the white colonial powers. I felt so sorry for them. It could almost be called 'Genocide with the best of intentions.'

Usually, when we were filming in any venue, we got to chat to the local people and exchange ideas, learn a bit more about their lives and get a general feel for their day to day activities. Not one of the San approached us, nor were there any offers of tea or hospitality. Even when we were shown inside one of the houses we were accompanied by the project manager, who pointed out the features. The rightful owners were nowhere in sight. It was a sad and depressing place and I was quite relieved when we finally climbed back into the car and drove away.

One of our trickiest challenges to shoot was to record meetings. Most finalists had compiled lists of actions to put into practice and getting everyone around a table was the best way of including the whole team so everyone would be featured in the video. Also none of the projects would even see the light of day unless it had all been formulated on paper first.

We would also insist that the tea lady and the cleaners were shown at some time somewhere in the background, intent on slamming home the concept that everyone worked together as a team and everyone had an important and necessary part to play. As far as I was concerned, the employee who supplied the coffee was the most important member of the team.

To start with this was not too difficult, but as time went on, the same shots of one long table, people sitting on chairs next to each other, with close up shots of hands holding pens, pencils, sheets of paper and so on, became really tedious.

We tried every which way to make these very boring scenes more interesting. Russell held the camera at 45 degrees, he climbed on chairs and took overhead shots, he tried over the shoulder shots from the participants' point of view, he even considered shots from below until I pointed out many of the ladies wore skirts.

I have to admire the composure of our subjects who calmly tried to ignore Russell as he climbed on cupboards, filing cabinets and side tables, or disappeared outside to shoot them through the window, but only if the office was on the ground floor, I insisted on that. They would go on discussing matters, doing their best to ignore us as Russell walked up and down the table, missing their fingers by inches as he took overhead shots of glasses of water and cups of cold coffee.

We had a difficult shoot in one province where many of the departments were in the government complex. As we drove in each day, the car had to be thoroughly searched, which meant unpacking all the equipment, opening our lunch time snacks, and allowing officials to peer into our bumbags and pat our pockets.

Once inside, we would stand and wait to be signed in by a member of the finalist team. This could take an hour or more and it stretched our patience to the limit as we were working to such a tight schedule.

The organising team for the awards would order the

venue, book the entertainment, decide on the food and drink, reserve the speakers, arrange accommodation for those from out of town and then, at the last minute think about the video and the booklet. It always seemed to happen that we were the last on the list to be contracted. So we were always given an impossible lead time to produce an hour-long showreel ready for the awards ceremony and that date, of course, was cast in stone.

One horrible morning, while yet another department kept us waiting, to save time, I suggested we get some extra external shots of the provincial government buildings which we could use to pop into several programmes. The exteriors and the gardens were very well kept, and the architecture gave us lots of scope for creative shots.

I don't know why I think it was done on purpose, but a couple of minutes later, a gardener appeared and turned his hose on us. We were so lucky the camera wasn't ruined, but it put everyone in a bad mood for the rest of the day.

I think it might have been the same day when our subject specialist took off, leaving vague directions as to where the elected project was. She was off shopping with a colleague. However, the message assured us they would be providing lunch at one of the top steak houses in the local mall and we should meet up round about two.

We finally parked up outside the restaurant almost an hour late, exhausted at having to shoot, research, interview and take the still photographs in such a short time, to find the whole management team feasting at the government's expense. Our camera stayed in its box.

As we entered, I was shocked to see a particular

government minister laughing and joking with the rest, enjoying the huge plate in front of her which was piled high with food. I was shocked, because the previous week she'd been exposed on national television for having ruthlessly abused her position. She had defrauded thousands of rand of government money by awarding contracts to unqualified companies run by family and friends. The case was so bad, that we understood she had been relieved of her duties, yet here she was, wining and dining, laughing and joking.

We were introduced and it was handshakes all round. I didn't know what to say and I found it difficult to look her in the eye. What did you say to a happy, disgraced government minister?

"Just how large is your bank account in the Cayman Islands?" sprang to mind, but was not really polite I guess.

When I had a moment alone with one of the team, whom I had got to know quite well, as we had shot in the province for several years, I asked about the minister's, well, 'delicate' situation.

"Oh it wasn't her fault," my new friend said, as we washed our hands in the ladies. "She didn't know what she was doing, now everyone is making such a fuss."

"She doesn't seem, uh, worried," I ventured tentatively.

"Oh no, she's being promoted next week. It's a much better job, more money and a bigger car, so she's quite happy." The awards organizer smiled at me as she dried her hands on a paper towel. And I honestly believed she was quite comfortable with the situation. Only in Africa? Possibly not.

Another problem I wrestled with was the political-speak in interviews. For example, police-speak would be:

"I was proceeding in an easterly direction along West Street at oh seven hundred hours on Saturday the ninth of December 2014, when I became aware of the accused in the act of perpetrating a crime. To wit one projectile..."

I'm sure you've heard that sort of thing on television dozens of times. For some reason quite unknown to me, the police don't say "I was walking along West Street about seven in the evening, when I noticed that guy in the defendant's cage, lobbing a bloody great brick through the jeweller's window."

It was the same with the politicians and government workers. Do they attend special speech classes?

"Please just explain what you have done in simple words," I would implore them, "as if you were chatting to your children at the breakfast table."

They would smile and nod and then say. "Under the government directive of 2001, we were empowered to provide habitable dwellings for a total of seventy-six per cent of the population who qualified under the redress scheme as promulgated by parliament, wherewith we undertook to prepare a feasibility study in conjunction with our ratified partners within the guidelines as set out in..."

I would take a deep breath and cry "Cut!"

I would smile sweetly and say. "Now can you try that again, and will you please say: 'After lots of planning with all the other departments, we are going to build new houses for all the people who qualify for them.'"

I would be met with blank stares, but we would try again.

"Various departmental heads and the teams under their jurisdiction have committed to providing the required levels of habitation for..."

"Cut!"

"Tell me what did you have for supper last night?"

"Pardon?"

"Did you eat out, or stay at home and eat in?"

"We went out, it was my daughter's birthday so the whole family went to McDonald's and we had..."

"Right," I would exclaim in triumph, "that's 'normal' speak! Remember this video will be shown to lots of people, and they are possibly not as well educated as you and don't understand the long words. So, that's how I want you to talk to me as you tell us about your project. Can we try it again?"

Most politicians and officials felt very uncomfortable having to explain their projects and achievements in ordinary, everyday language. They might well have suspected that the average man in the street could now really understand what they were promising, or reporting on, and might hold them to account at some stage in the future.

On the other hand I often wondered if they were so immersed in their own 'government speak', that they actually lost sight of what they were trying to do.

As the years went on, I would ask the interviewee to explain the topic, or what they wanted to say. They would rabbit on for a couple of moments before I could get a word in to stop them, and then I would condense down the whole lot into a couple of sentences and ask them to repeat these to camera.

A young trainee who was with us on one occasion, was

shocked and asked why I was telling our spokespersons what to say, surely that wasn't right? I was putting words into their mouths! Wasn't I subverting the truth? (Well, if you have read this far, you will understand I had been doing that on many occasions, well, skirting around it certainly.) But this wasn't an example of that.

I told her that I was only asking them to repeat what they'd already told me in simple language that everyone could understand. It saved tempers, it saved time and ultimately, it saved money too. We used less tape!

There was also the problem of what we call 'red light fever'. There is a small light on the front of the camera which glows red when the tape is rolling, and often a confident interviewee would be quite ready to speak until they saw the light go on. Then they dried up and stood there, mouth opening and closing like a goldfish, issuing the odd gurgled sound. We solved this problem quite easily, by disabling the light, but I would have to remember to check with Russell that it was a good take. We had a secret sign language which would let me know when the tape was running so I would know what we had recorded without letting on to the interviewee. Very often we recorded the final interview during our *practice* session which made the whole procedure less painful for everyone.

Often I did not have the chance to 'suggest' phrases to important persons as they were addressing large crowds of people. I'm sure that most of their audience didn't understand a word, but such is the awe held for chiefs, government officials and representatives of large corporations, the patient African would sit on the bare, dusty ground and listen silently for hours under the sweltering hot sun.

Occasionally we met a few Steven Spielberg wannabes on our travels, who knew exactly what shots they wanted. Sometimes they would not only point and try to direct the cameraman, they would insist on looking at the shots we had and spend precious time checking we had the right angles and lighting. They would cheerfully thump Russell on the shoulder to indicate the next shot, ruining the one he was focusing on at the time. They would also insist in writing the script and argue fiercely against including the tea lady in the shot, or any other personnel they might not like.

There was always great competition to be included in any shots, and it took a lot of tact to persuade the head of a department to get off the camera and allow another member of his staff to say a few words as well.

"It's a team effort," I would remind them, "and it will show everyone that you all work together happily to do the best for your clients."

Reluctantly they would usually agree, but on one occasion this backfired on me as there were only three members in this project team, one of them had a particularly bad stammer and the other was too shy to say anything at all!

My varied experiences gave me plenty of anecdotes for the classes I was lecturing when it came to interview techniques. If you are well prepared, then you might have a couple of questions lined up, such as the interviewee's name and secondly where he or she lived. If the first reply included the name and town of residence, then for heaven's sake skip question two and move on! I've seen this on television, honestly, and it's both hysterical and embarrassing!

Interviewer: "So, can you tell me your name?"

Interviewee: "I'm Mrs Macube and I live just over there in the township."

Interviewer: "And where do you live?"

Interviewee: "Uh, um, over there in the township. I run a small spaza shop next to my house."

Interviewer: "And what work do you do? Do you have to travel far to work and do you take a local taxi?"

Interviewee: "What? But I just told you..."

I know it sounds ridiculous but it happens, and it's broadcast.

There also seems a propensity for interviewers, especially in Britain, to spend time talking about themselves, giving their own views and asking questions, only to give the answer themselves. This leaves the real interviewee no chance to say anything and he or she only gets to nod occasionally in agreement, seldom getting a word in edgeways. I'm not sure why they bother bringing in the experts on many occasions, we hear so very little from them.

12 AWARDS & BANQUETS

Most of our work did not have large budgets, so there was no hiring tracks and dollies and retaking shots to get 30 seconds in the can each day. We learned to improvise. Supermarket trolleys can work just as well, as long as the ground is smooth. Many a time people have stopped and stared in amazement, as we stuffed the cameraman into the trolley, then wheeled him around the store or along the street.

I was lucky in South Africa as we were free to go and shoot just about anywhere, except in restaurants, and I have been thrown out of a couple of shopping malls for not getting permission first. But generally, no one minded if you went out to take crowd shots, or panned along shop fronts, or recorded people at the races or on the beach, and I thought this was all quite normal.

Until the day I was hired as a production assistant when the skateboarder Tony Hawk flew over from the United States to open the new park at the Gateway Shopping Mall. They were making a series for American television about his life and his achievements in the world of skateboarding. As he'd designed the large facility at our enormous shopping centre, he was the most obvious celebrity to declare it well and truly open.

At the pre-production meeting I was handed a sheet of

paper and asked to copy it 50 times and make sure it was put up in all the areas that would be used during the programme. It informed the public what was going on, and in so many words, warned them that if they did not wish to be seen they were to keep well away from the cameras. The company would take no responsibility and could not be sued in the event anyone might be seen in the background.

This was my introduction to the new privacy laws which I know have spread to the United Kingdom. Now you need written permission from each and everyone before you roll the camera. So if you've ever wondered why you get so many shots of feet tramping along the pavement, or fuzzed out faces on the children in the playground or people walking down the street, now you know why.

It's probably the same in South Africa these days, and several of the larger towns now have a film office which in theory is there to help you with locations and logistics. The reality is the staff is sitting there ready and willing to charge you for using the town as your backdrop. It costs megabucks and involves masses of red tape and paperwork to have areas cleared and roads closed, when in the old days, a quick call to the local police gave us a day's filming for nothing. It was all part of the job, and the lucky guy on point duty would join in the action if he could and have a great day out being part of the movie.

I remember one fun shoot to advertise the launch of a new newspaper published in Zulu, where we used a taxi. The driver stopped to pick up a newspaper and we then cut to the inside of his vehicle to see the passengers all fighting to try and read it. It was a comedy sketch, my favourite medium, and we had the road closed off for the whole day. It didn't cost us a cent. We only had to make sure we included the policemen who were helping us divert the traffic, they insisted on that!

I think it's a shame that small video companies like mine are now so worried about court action and being sued. Just how paranoid has the world become?

I would get cross with the crew though when the background crowd called out, "When will it be on television?"

"Tomorrow night, channel two!" they would reply.

"Don't be so mean! You know that's not true!" I would complain. But the crew just couldn't resist it. If it wasn't going to be on television then it wasn't important and you lost a lot of status.

When the American crew went back to Tony Hawk's hotel room to capture a few words to camera, I was amazed at the amount of equipment they had with them. I don't know how much of it they had flown across the Atlantic, but you would think they were lighting the Olympic opening ceremony. They fiddled around for ages to get interesting shapes and shadows and different effects in a variety of colours on the wall behind him. They opened and closed the barn doors on the blondes and the redheads (referring to the lights) chopping and changing the coloured gels over the bulbs and took so long, I began to doze off.

I was amazed to see that in the end, they filmed him in such a tight close up that you couldn't even see the artistically lit background behind him.

Different filming techniques have come and gone and older people may remember a time when it became all the rage to shoot very, very close to the subject so the whole screen was filled with one eye and one nostril – it's called a very big close up or VBCU. This was followed by the shaky camera era when tripods must have been in short supply, and the swaying motion as we followed the action was enough to make you seasick.

Then there was the 'quick fire' craze which swung the camera from one character to the next, making the viewer feel as if they were watching a Wimbledon match where the players were on speed.

I was never sure if these 'interesting' techniques were introduced to cover up a weak script, appalling acting, or desperation on the part of the cinematographer to make his mark and collect awards. Thankfully, all these fads seemed to have faded into the background and we are back to the straight cuts between shots, which, if you watch any classic, black and white movie, was the way they used to film. They got it right the first time.

Well we must have been doing something right as we were asked year after year by the Provincial governments to tender to shoot the finalists for the upcoming awards.

As you can imagine, filming up to twelve finalists in seven different provinces year after year could get a little boring. Not filming the shortlisted candidates, nor the travelling, although that was tiring, but the way of presenting them differently each time. After the first couple, I had to come up with a theme to hang them altogether.

One year we had a picture gallery, where each painting

on the art gallery wall came to life. I had children introducing the segments saying that this is what the winners were doing for their future. For another province I turned the programme into a news broadcast and introduced them that way. I can't honestly remember them all now, but my favourite one was the traditional story teller, sitting in the Valley of a Thousand Hills, with the story of modern heroes of Africa, who were, yes, you've guessed it, the finalists. As our presenter turned each page, we brought it to life. To my delight Gcina Mhlope agreed to play the part. I had never forgotten this amazing storyteller from when *Heinemann* had sent me on the '*Read Writing*' course in Johannesburg all those years ago. What made it even better, she herself lived just outside Durban and I suggested to the organisers that she should also be the compère for the awards banquet.

They were rather taken aback, arguing that we could not use someone who was famous in Johannesburg for a show in Durban. Since at least half the musicians and singers were being brought down from the Reef, I couldn't see that it was a problem.

I know that often they engaged a member of the awards committee on the government side to run the evening and act as Master of Ceremonies, and usually they were a disaster! They were not performers and they read through the script as if it was a bus timetable.

Finally after much debate, they agreed, and Gcina gave an amazing performance, bringing a new hype to the occasion, interspersed with short tales and switching from English to Zulu, to Xhosa with ease.

There were two other speakers who really impressed

me when they stood up to address the audience. One was the then premier of the Northern Cape. He had simply entered the awards venue without bodyguards or praise singers and right on time. He stopped to chat and shake hands with many of the ordinary people and when he made his speech, his words were sensible, non-divisive and full of hope for the future.

I heard a similar speech later that year, by the man who was very involved in the Airports Company in South Africa. I'd just finished a programme for them on the re-vamping of the old Durban airport, which seemed a bit daft as they had every intention of building the new King Shaka airport on the other side of town in the very near future.

I thought the re-vamp made a big difference, and why they wanted another airport I wasn't sure. There were some mutterings about the runway sinking, or wanting to extend the harbour, but whatever the reason, it was another excuse for a great party.

I was amazed that this time I was invited as a guest and I didn't even have to film anything, that's how nice our client was! As he stood up to speak, my admiration grew and I turned to the person sitting next to me to share my enthusiasm.

"Yes, we will miss him, he's done a lot of good work," he replied.

"Oh, is he going somewhere?"

"Possibly to jail, but even if he manages to stay out he can't continue to work. They may deport him."

"But why?" I was amazed and disappointed. "What's he done wrong?"

"He hasn't got the right papers, it appears as if he is not South African, and he forged his qualifications."

With the new 'reverse apartheid' in mind, this was a surprise. The speaker was an African and it was obvious his ancestors had lived in Africa long before the Dutch had set up their refreshment station at the Cape. What I'm trying to say poetically here is that he was black.

I never did get to the bottom of what was wrong with his paperwork, a degree he didn't have or forged residence papers or passport, who knows? It might have been something quite different and I am only guessing but, like a few others crying in the wilderness, he believed in everyone working together for the good of each other.

It was something very close to my heart, and somewhere along the way someone called us the '*Rainbow Crew*' and it stuck, one white, one Indian and one black African. We had our differences but we all had the same goal, to film and record and meet our deadlines while delivering the best possible programmes. We also became the very best of friends.

After a couple of years filming good customer services for the provincial governments, the local cities and towns climbed on board and decided to hold similar awards competitions of their own. If I was really uncharitable, I would think that part of the attraction was the celebration banquet when the finalists were announced.

These were lavish affairs, and recording the event was part of the package deal. Afterwards, we would edit the highlights and tack these onto the end of the finalists' video. It was a good opportunity to showcase all the important and famous people from each municipality dressed up in all their finery.

Another part of my job was to write the speeches for many of the important people, plus the script for the compère or master of ceremonies and compile the running order of events.

I was a bit taken aback when I was asked to include a message from the podium at the end of the evening that the guests were forbidden from taking home the plates, cutlery, silverware and the table decorations. They were only allowed to remove the balloons and their place cards. This didn't always stop them though. Often a sedate and impressive evening's entertainment was ruined by the indecent rush to pocket everything in sight that was not nailed down.

On one occasion at the Durban Playhouse when they were showcasing all the new programmes to be used in schools the following year, I watched in horror as the invited teachers opened their handbags and swept in large quantities of food to take home. In went the sausage rolls, cream cupcakes, pâté on biscuits and egg mayonnaise sandwiches all tumbled in together. What state these foods were in when the bag owners arrived home, I dread to think.

I have always been a fan of the comedian Dave Alan and liked the way he said at the end of the programme "And may your God go with you." I liked the all-encompassing, non-judgemental words and, imitation being the sincerest form of flattery, I always wrote this in as the final words of the evening. On each and every occasion it was removed and no one ever said why.

I was asked on a couple of occasions to direct rehearsals, which was not exactly my forte. It was all very well getting the floor staff to stand in as the premier or an important guest, and manhandle the winners into a line suitable for having their still pictures taken. But, when the real people arrived (when they finally pitched up) they had no idea where to stand and didn't follow the rules anyway. Often the stage manager and her assistants were so star struck they totally forgot what to do.

We would of course have a plan of what and where to shoot during the evening, and we were clued up to show as much of the premier, or mayor, sponsors and honoured guests as possible. It was a bit tricky with the sponsors as we hadn't a clue what they looked like and could only hope the place cards on the tables told us where they would be sitting. We passed round pictures of all the important people we knew to everyone, especially the cameramen. This was fine for the men, but not so easy for the women, especially if they turned up in wigs.

We also needed to highlight the winners, this was their evening after all, and while we may have filmed them labouring in some far-flung field wearing their working clothes, when they arrived for the gala evening it was very hard to recognise them at all. We were treated to a wonderful display of African couture, with towering headdresses, swirling skirts and elegant accessories. The quantities of jewellery were also spectacular as these ladies jangled and sashayed to their places.

I thought it a shame that the hard-working finalists were only allocated four or six invitations for the whole team to attend, while the numbers for the celebrities, friends and family of the government people, sponsors and advertisers were seemingly unlimited.

No expense was spared in holding these lavish spectacles. Event organisers were hired, some excellent and some abysmal. International guest acts were engaged and the venue was decked out with all the bells and whistles for a four course feast. Most times we were fed as well, but not always, and sometimes we watched in envy as the guests tucked into exotic dishes while we accosted the delivery boy at the back of the venue and chomped our pizzas sitting on the floor hidden below the production table.

These were great opportunities to meet our finalists again and they usually came round to say hello, (even the lady from the deep rural school set in the midst of the canals. I had difficulty in recognising her since she had taken out her hair curlers!)

We used three or four cameras on those evenings, and on later shoots we had a boom camera set up as well.

The trickiest part was recording the initial reaction from the finalists, as they still didn't know who had won the gold, silver or bronze awards. The moment a camera approached their table they would get all fired up, as they had seen on the big screens the close up shots of the next ones to be called up. We learned to be very sneaky about this so as not to spoil the surprise.

We also had to fight for our space with the crews from the television networks who turned up at the last minute. Our crew had often travelled several hundred kilometres to the venue, slept nearby overnight, and then spent the whole day setting up all the equipment, the cameras, the large screens, the rear projectors, the mixing desk and so on. We would naturally choose the optimum place for everything, but we had to be on our guard. A couple of minutes before the show started, crews from the news channels would barrel in and try to take over our space, and that could not be allowed. On one occasion a particularly nasty gentleman set up his camera right in front of ours. All you could see through our lens was him, bending over his lens!

On these occasions I would bear down like the avenging angel and ask them politely to move, but sometimes they would appear halfway through the show, just to record the top three trophies being presented. It was much harder to dislodge them then!

We were often quite naughty during shows, especially when the speeches droned on and on and on, often on a self-congratulating political theme. We were all in radio mike contact, wearing earphones and we would often laugh and joke and make comments about both speaker and audience.

We had a huge emergency right before one award ceremony. We'd set up the equipment to shoot the show, had the video featuring all the finalists in the machine and we were all ready to roll when one of the organisers approached us in a panic.

"You will have to change the video," she wailed.

"Change it? But we can't!" we replied. "It's all on disk, and the music and the voice are all synced in and it's sort of locked together now."

"It has to be changed," she insisted. "The piece on the 'Eye Care Project', you can see a sponsor's banner in it!"

"Yes, we know. The subject specialist asked us to include it as they have collected massive funds for the project."

"No, they didn't, well not for the Eye Care people." said our distraught official, "They embezzled the lot and disappeared with all the money! They *must* be removed."

This was the first of two occasions when we had to direct a four-camera recording of a live show, and re-edit at the same time on limited equipment. I had to creep down the side of the venue with alternate directions for the cameramen, and hunt frantically for footage we could insert for the shot we took out. To this day I have no idea why I had decided to bring the original source tapes 700 kilometres to the show, but it saved our bacon that night.

At another show, just as we were ready to start, with the audience all in place sitting quietly chatting, we received word that the premier of that province was just boarding a plane 800 kilometres away. I counted on my fingers and realised that it was going to take him at least an hour and a half to two hours flying time, even if they went like the clappers. But then the airfield was another 12 kilometres from the venue, so we had a minimum of three hours to wait for him.

Luckily the organisers hijacked a guest in the audience who was known for his excellent stand-up comedy routine, but even he had trouble stretching his repertoire for three hours. We were all tired too, as we'd been up since dawn. There was absolutely no possibility we could start without the premier, it was his show and his awards.

So we waited and waited and waited, even the praise singer, resplendent in his furs, dozed off in a corner. But these things happen, and we would just have to be patient. That was fine, except for the fact that when the guest of honour finally arrived, he spent a further 20 odd minutes chatting to people in the foyer. Now that did make me angry.

OK, so it's a sign in African culture that the more important you are the longer you can keep people waiting. But when you have over five hundred other important people waiting, the caterers tearing their hair out trying to keep the food edible, the costs for the suppliers going into overtime, and the entertainers panicking they would not get the last plane back to Johannesburg, surely you could *pretend* to hurry? There is a balance between being important and simple, plain manners. No such luck, this man knew just how important he was. I wonder if he noticed the veiled hostility he encountered from a good section of the audience when he finally made his entrance.

However, his late arrival did have a positive spin-off for me, as I got chatting to the manager of the soon-to-be opened Hilton Hotel in Durban. I'd always been curious how you got a new enterprise up and running, well I'm curious about almost anything. He mentioned that just before they officially open, they invite a few people in to stay over and note down all the snags and give a report back. You have already guessed who volunteered haven't you?

The following weekend my husband and I were whisked up in the lift to the sixth floor, and unpacked our bags before being treated to a divine dinner in the lavish new restaurant. It felt a little surreal staying in a hotel in our own home town, our house was barely 20 kilometres away, but at least two hours were spent filling in a plethora of forms.

While one dressing gown and only three slippers were there for the use of, they neglected to provide any towels. These were finally delivered the following morning, which we carefully noted down on the questionnaire. In general we had a great stay, but were highly amused to hear that the guests invited to occupy the main suite on the top floor had complained bitterly that their microwave was not working.

The night manager apologised profusely, promised to sort it out straight away and he was about to phone the engineering department, when he suddenly remembered that the Hilton did not provide microwave ovens in any of their rooms. He raced upstairs to find out what the problem was to be met by the irate couple who were cradling a raw chicken. He was told they had put it in the cooker over an hour ago and the damned bird was still raw. The guests had been trying to cook their supper in the room safe.

I was only once involved in stage managing a simultaneous live and recorded show for broadcast. Since Durban has the largest Indian population in any city outside of India, there was an annual 'ment of' *Miss India South Africa*' beauty pageant. The winner would then compete in the '*Miss India Worldwide*' finals held in a different overseas country each year.

It is always held at the Durban Playhouse, a well-equipped theatre, complete with drop stage, orchestra pit and large backstage areas. From the start that year's contest was a bit of a disaster as the opening act, a famous singer, found himself on the wrong side of the stage. I was receiving instructions in my earpiece from the outside broadcast van parked in the street to, "Cut and start again!" But when I tried to do that I was over-ruled by the 'live' stage manager, who was not going to re-do anything in front of a packed house of specially invited and important guests. So while the producer from outside was shouting obscenities in one ear, I heard plenty more in the other ear from the producer inside the theatre. I stepped back to try and manhandle our singer round to the correct side of the stage and fell against a young lady who was standing right behind me.

"Why don't you f*** off," I snarled at her, stumbling over her foot. "What the hell are you doing here anyway? Get out of the wings!"

Well how was I to know she was last year's winner, waiting there to hand over the crown to her successor? What made it even worse, I had stood heavily on her foot and when the time came for her regal entrance, she was hobbling like a 90 year old, and managed to knock over a small hedge on her way across the stage.

When we began shooting the municipal awards we were off back around the country again. In one province we were given such very short notice, I had to hire in two extra crews, and as we all drove north, I received the information that they wanted to throw in some youth awards as well. It seemed that award fever was sweeping the nation. We were going to be flying in all directions and it called for rapid planning.

I thought it was an excellent idea to highlight young

people who were making it in the entrepreneurial world, although I did have my doubts about a couple of them. In one location the young man refused to allow us to show his actual premises, we must just show the close ups of his paint spraying company in action. And no, we were not to show all of the vehicle he was working on either, especially the part where the company logo was – it wasn't his company logo, he was busy covering it up with paint. I was convinced we were in a chop-shop, a place where stolen cars are received, dismantled for parts, or altered and sold on.

We were close to an international border, and it would have been so easy to pop them across, then north into the rest of Africa. Now this enterprising youth was getting a prestigious award for running such a successful business. I wondered who'd nominated him.

Since we only had a few days to edit the three inserts we were shooting each day, I had hired in two editors and we all travelled several hundred kilometres north. There would be no time to return to Durban to edit, so while the crews were out shooting the footage, Brian and his assistant would be putting the previous day's programmes together on a portable edit suite in the guest house. I was a bit horrified the second night to discover how little they had done, they were still on the first one! The other editor I'd not worked with before was a total perfectionist and quite brilliant at her job, but in circumstances like this, we didn't have the luxury of spending two hours on a few seconds of final footage. This was not Hollywood.

They worked much faster the second day, but there were still five inserts to put together the night before the show. They promised to work through the night if necessary.

I could never, ever, complain about any of the crew who worked with me. They gave their all, everyone functioned as a team and there were never any harsh words. No one ever asked for overtime pay, it was always a flat rate for the project, and sometimes they could knock off early, sometimes we were there well past midnight and into the early hours of the morning.

However, on this occasion, the will to work through the night backfired, badly! We had just decided to go and get a quick meal before getting back to work, when there was an almighty crack of thunder, the heavens opened and all the lights went out. The owner of the guest house where we were staying assured us that this happened frequently, and often they were without power for hours, sometimes even days.

The 'days' part was fine as I doubted the venue had a separate power source and that meant the event might be cancelled. But the 'hours' part was not so good, as there was no chance of working on the video until the power came back on.

We decided to go out and eat anyway, maybe there was electricity in other parts of the town. That was a big mistake. The city we were in had been the capital of one of the designated homeland areas in apartheid days, which meant it was a self-governing region which made its own decisions and ran its own affairs.

At no point had anyone suggested that storm water outlets were a good idea, so no one had put any in. As a result, while we thought it would be easy to drive into town, we discovered roads ankle deep in dark, swirling water. Luckily one of our crew vehicles was a four wheel drive SUV and we let that go first, because there had been very few repairs made to the roads for years and the potholes were truly horrendous. Shallow puddles that looked passable were quite impossible for an ordinary saloon to negotiate. Several times we were forced to turn round as we met large lakes spread across the roads and pavements. We could not tell where one began and the other ended. We had no map either and this was in those far-off days when GPS devices were things of the future.

Eventually, we found a burger-type takeaway and instead of a proper meal, we had to make do with a stale bun and a bit of mashed up meat and pickle at an exorbitant price.

It was just as big a battle to get back to the guest house as by now the water had reached knee height in places. We all had an early night, but I did not sleep, I tossed and turned wondering what I was going to say the next day when the show began and the video was not ready to play. How angry would the client be? In seven years this had never happened before, and I knew it was no good trying to tell them they had not given us enough time to complete the work successfully. But then it was also my fault for accepting the project and undertaking to get it finished on time. I would still have to pay all the expenses for three crews and this could wipe me out financially.

I guess, looking back now, I did not run my little company in a very businesslike way. I'd worked with big production companies in Johannesburg who had legal documents showing each stage of production and required the clients to sign off at each milestone. It was a great idea, but sometimes I was only able to see the client briefly at the beginning of the project and then we were off on location, driving all over the province. As soon as we had finished, we would race straight back to Durban and fling ourselves into the edit studio. There wasn't enough time to breathe, let alone liaise with the clients at every stage.

The clients themselves were much too busy to bother with us anyway. They were running around organising the big banquet, wining and dining each other and generally having a great time.

On one occasion I was even brave enough, or foolish enough, to begin a shoot without getting the fifty per cent deposit up front. I was told I was an idiot, but as it was a provincial government I had worked for previously, and I had forged links with the organizers, I took the chance. There would not have been enough shooting and edit days if the crew had not jumped in the car and set off when we did.

Sometimes at the end of the day's shooting, if we were working in the capital city, I would go into the payments office and ask plaintively if the cheque was ready yet. I was always paid, and the one business principle I kept to was to have enough cash flow to fund the beginning of the next project.

However, I always consoled myself with the thought that if my back was right against the wall, I could, on the afternoon of the awards day, simply refuse to hand over the video if I had not been paid at least the first fifty per cent. It never actually came to that, but it was always at the back of my mind, as long as I could find the courage to even make such a threat.

I mentioned earlier that I could not have wished for a better team, it would be difficult to find another crowd of people who were so passionate and committed to doing the very best job they could.

I think the secret of keeping the company afloat was that I always paid all crew members as soon as the edit was completed, which included the banquet footage. By not paying myself, and carefully managing the funds I had available, I was able to settle a lot of accounts immediately the shoot was over.

I was even less business-like about insurance (besides the camera itself) I never had any. Talk about trusting to luck!

Anyway back to our rain-sodden situation. At the venue the following day, as half the crew set up, the editors, who were usually involved in plugging in cables and setting up the screens and so on, were still editing at lunch time. Sadly at this stage I was no help at all. I can use a camera, but don't ask me to do anything technical. I can be relied on to jam things in the wrong places, or wire stuff back to front and blow up the lot. I'm not even very good at rolling cables.

My job that morning was to keep the clients as far away from our control desk as possible. I didn't dare let them see we were still working on putting the video together and that no, we were not ready to go. Luckily they had enough problems of their own, rescuing banners and posters which had been ruined in the rain and panicking that, due to the weather, the honoured guests who'd been invited might not show after all.

Yes, we did finish in time and I was very impressed with the way we had recorded the 'chop-shop', it looked almost legitimate!

13 THE FINAL WRAP

Each time we put a programme together, the graphics and the audio were just that bit better. As the technology moved forward, we moved with it. The graphics were now more sophisticated. I began writing for split screens featuring several scenes at once, which allowed me to showcase more of each finalist. It was almost time to retire our large, ancient camera and dive in with the new HD models.

These were small, light and more manoeuvrable and I could now carry several spare tapes in my bum bag. My career now spread over into a third generation of equipment, and each time it got smaller and smaller. We had space in the car for two cameras, and the largest thing we had to cart around was the tripod.

If our hosts were unimpressed by the small crew that pitched up to spend a day with them, they were even more dismayed by the miniature equipment, and I think we lost a bit of respect as the latest state of the art camera now looked like an original box brownie.

I was so privileged to see so much of the country, and gain countless insights into the lives led by ordinary people, and be welcomed into their homes, and learn about the harsh reality of life. But there were times when I longed for a little more glamour. It was often hard while so many of my colleagues seemed to be having a great time.

"Just back from the Caribbean, for a series on exotic hotels, it was brilliant."

"It was great in Singapore, a real experience."

"We're doing a piece on people who have moved to the States and we'll be travelling all over North America."

"Off to Australia next week, can't wait. What are you working on, Lucinda?"

"Uh, a school and an abattoir just north of here, and then I have a series on urine diversion toilets in the informal townships." It just didn't carry the same thrilling appeal somehow.

Don't get me wrong, I loved my work, and I was earning a good living, but sometimes, just sometimes, I wished I could go somewhere exotic too. I thought my chance had finally come when a producer phoned me and asked if I would fly up to Maputo, the capital of Mozambique, to research and write the script for the new aluminium plant up there. Wow, now was my chance! International travel, all expenses paid. What a dream!

As I waited for Paul the director at the airport, I looked in envy at the destination boards. Paris, London, Mauritius, Perth, New York, and where was I going? Mozambique, just a hop across the border, but I was not about to complain. This might be the start of some serious international travel! It wasn't, but let's not go there right? I was still hoping at that time.

As the large, thundering planes took off, I noticed a very tiny plane waiting on the tarmac. That was the one *we* were booked on. I had serious doubts it was large enough to hold sufficient fuel to get us that far north, but at least it had two engines, I adore flying, but I like a spare engine just in case. The director arrived and we walked out to board the plane.

When we landed at Maputo, as usual everyone stood up and started bunching in the aisle to get off, none of this, 'Please wait until the plane has come to a complete standstill before releasing your safety belts' nonsense. We were seasoned travellers and we were all ready, luggage in hand, to disembark as quickly as possible.

I rather wished I had stayed in my seat, as we stood and we stood and we stood, and no one seemed to know what the holdup was.

Please don't tell me that the civil war has broken out again, I prayed, not right at the start of my international career, that would be too unkind.

When we finally shuffled forward, it was to find that the rain was pouring down in stair rods and each passenger had to wait his or her turn to be escorted across the tarmac by the air hostess (whoops that should be flight attendant) one at a time, under an umbrella. The moment you put a foot on the ground, the water swirled high over your ankles, but she was doing her very best to keep the rest of us as dry as possible, at least from the knees up.

Despite the fact we said we were quite willing to make a dash for it, she was adamant that we had to remain at the top of the steps until she returned with the umbrella. I think it took longer to offload the plane one at a time, than the actual flight.

Maputo was a sad place. Although it was in the early stage of recovery from the war, the signs were still there. Bullet holes in the walls, craters in the road. A four by four was recommended to get anywhere, even around the suburbs. You could still see where fires had broken out from the blackened buildings with gaping holes where once there had been windows and doors. It reminded me of the pictures I'd seen of the bomb sites in London after the World War II.

Our guest house was very basic, but at one time, it must have been an imposing mansion, with beautiful gardens. The conversion was rough, and what had once been a grand reception room was now a kind of bar, dining room and pool hall. How delightful, I thought.

I was alarmed to see how many candles they had left in the bedroom, next to a gigantic box of matches. They were obviously expecting power cuts and in the three days we were there we must have had at least five or six. There were notices not to open the windows due to the swarms of mosquitoes, and everyone knew there was an added danger if bitten, since the arrival of a dangerous malarial strain which attacked the brain.

Like many people who have lived in Africa for a long time, I never took prophylactic medicines against malaria, as they could mask the symptoms and not give you total protection. If you contracted the disease, even in its early stages, it was easier for the doctor to diagnose and treat you effectively. Of course, it was best not to get bitten at all, so I sprayed myself from top to toe before I went down to dinner.

The menu looked quite extensive and there was a wide range of dishes on offer.

"I'll have the steak and chips please." I was hungry by now and one juice on the plane was not enough to fill me up.

"Not available," replied the waiter.

"Right, the chicken breast then, please,"

"Not available," he repeated.

"What about the *boeuf stroganoff?*"

"Not available, no beef."

"Right, so that eliminates the stew, and the beef cordon bleu, and the ribs?"

"No, not available."

Paul cut in, "What do you have?"

"Beef burgers."

"And what else?"

"Beef burgers."

"Just beef burgers?"

"Yes."

Paul looked at me and I nodded. "Then we better have beef burgers for two please."

The waiter picked up the menus and disappeared in the direction of the kitchen. Why he didn't just say they were short of food and tell us what was on offer in the first place, I did not even try to guess. Maybe he wanted us to appreciate what they *could* provide if they could get the ingredients. I didn't like to think the cook only knew how to prepare beef burgers and chips.

I also wondered, if there was no beef available, what the beef burgers were made of.

When the food arrived a better description would be old tyres pretending to be beef burgers. They were tough and rubbery, barely warm and they smelled a little under the weather as well. But we were ravenous and it's amazing what you can force down if you are hungry enough, although I have to admit the chef did make very nice chips. We agreed to find somewhere else to eat the following night.

We were collected the next morning by a cheerful employee from the aluminium plant, who couldn't wait to show us their new three lane highway. I don't think it was longer than about 20 kilometres at that time, and even that part was tolled, but surprise surprise, it led from the city right past the aluminium plant and not much further.

I had already researched and scripted a programme on the aluminium plant in Richard's Bay in South Africa, so I knew the basic procedure of how aluminium was produced. It was a fascinating place to visit. I have always loved watching mass production in action.

I was a bit curious why a huge multi-international company had invested millions of dollars in a plant for which a constant and reliable supply of electricity was vital. We had already suffered three power cuts and we'd only been there a couple of hours! I knew that to make aluminium, you heated it to fantastically high temperatures in a little pot. Should the electricity supply go off for any reason, the raw aluminium would solidify very quickly and each and every pot would have to be scraped out by hand. There were thousands of pots set up in long lines and these lines stretched off way into the distance. The best method of getting around was in a golf cart – which incidentally could also double up for those tracks and dollies for smooth, moving shots.

I wondered if the highly erratic power supply in the city occurred as the result of having to feed this hungry monster which devoured electricity nonstop each and every day of the year.

We had a very enjoyable tour round the plant and were so relieved when they offered us lunch, as breakfast had been appropriately sparse, a small bowl of cereal which arrived on the plate with one slice of toast each, while the coffee only pretended to be coffee.

At the end of the day we had decided to persuade our driver to drop us off at a restaurant in town, but he shook his head. It was not safe, and no, we could not take a taxi back, that was not safe either. He was following his instructions to the letter and dropped us back outside our less than luxurious hotel.

We had not expected to go through the same ritual with the waiter again that evening, as he handed us each a menu with such a happy smile and stood waiting with pad and pen poised to write down our order. It was an easy mistake for us to think that they'd had a delivery or two during the day.

It reminded me of a Monty Python routine as we asked for various items on the menu, but it appeared that all of them were unavailable. In fact nothing was available except, you've guessed it, beef burgers and chips.

By the third night I was dreading going down to the dining room, but Paul and I seemed to be the only ones complaining. Half the population of Maputo was crowded into the games room cum dining room cum lounge, playing pool and gorging themselves on beef burgers and chips. There appeared to be an unending supply of those. The noise was so loud it was impossible for us to have a conversation, so we retired early.

That was the sum total of my exotic travel in the video industry, three days in a war-ridden city, living off rubberised beef burgers and swatting mosquitoes before they had their lunch.

I wrote two programmes featuring the aluminium plant in Richard's Bay, though one was not so much on the production as on the safety aspect. As it was directed at the workers to encourage safe practices, I wrote it as short inserts following those employees who had not taken precautions to keep themselves safe. I was back on the docu-drama road again, with visual cautionary tales to scare the life out of any worker there who didn't follow the rules.

There was the blind man who had suffered severe electric shock. We saw his long suffering wife watching him try to feed himself as he smeared maize porridge all over his face. This was followed by the father who could no longer play football with his son. He sat in his wheelchair, swathed in bandages and cried loudly. There was also the boy who went fishing with his father and kept punching him on the shoulder, maybe hoping he would talk, but dad was no longer compos mentis, he just sat there in a dazed stupor. And the tragedy did not stop there. Enter a little girl crying (not very convincingly even I have to admit) by her father's grave after he drowned, and let's not forget the quadriplegic who had driven too fast on the company's roads and... Actually I can't remember what fate I dreamed up for him, but he wasn't enjoying life, I'm sure about that!

I was not involved in the production of this programme, but the acting was way, way over the top. I didn't think it would convey the message to anyone with half a brain cell, and when I used it as an example of a training video to my college students they fell about laughing and even I had trouble keeping a straight face.

But, you know, that video worked! The company told us it had been the most successful training programme ever and the accident rate fell dramatically. Yes, it reminded me of the Keystone Cops, and maybe it made the audience laugh, but it fulfilled its aims and objectives. At the end of the day, that made it a success.

In between all this government and municipal work we also produced the occasional insert for television. In their wisdom, the important powers that be in the SABC in Johannesburg, graciously allowed two of the provinces to broadcast their own half hour programme every weekday evening, with items of regional interest.

This was really quite brave in a way, as there was paranoia from Johannesburg about having uncontrolled broadcasting to the masses. In previous years it had taken a lot of hard talking and red tape, for the Durban City Council to obtain a ten week in-house licence from the government. Broadcasting over the peak holiday season at Christmas, *Beach Wise Radio* focused only on safe and healthy practices while on holiday, providing strictly non-political entertainment.

When the SABC in Durban were given the freedom to air their own 30 minute programme, they began to look for ideas.

My equipment partner Brian, hit on the idea of the evening joke, just a minute or even less, for one person talking to the camera to tell a non-racist, non-sexist, non-upset-anyone joke just to round off the evening's switch over.

Great idea, easy to set up, and so easy to persuade people to come and tell the jokes. All went well at first and we had them queuing up at the door to take part. This was going to be their fifteen milliseconds of fame, and who knows who might be watching and whisk them off to stardom?

But as the series progressed, people began to get cold feet and the jokes became decidedly questionable, even though we had vetted them first. Just as we were getting desperate Johannesburg pulled the plug on the whole programme and broadcasting at 6pm every night reverted to the main SABC studios in the commercial capital.

On another occasion, to put bread on the table, we pitched for a community affairs programme and they commissioned us to make inserts for them. They didn't want the complete programme, just the script and the raw footage, neatly logged. The pay wasn't great, and the only way we could make a reasonable profit was to shoot three inserts in one day.

We were on the road by five am recording the local fishermen down on one of Durban's piers, finding out how they made a living by selling their catch. We were a little uncomfortable to learn that they were disposing of their fish illegally, and many of the poor marine creatures were well undersized.

Hoping no one would notice these discrepancies, we next raced 80 kilometres up the freeway to film a shelter for wayward boys. That was quite traumatic, as they had some horrific stories to tell about gang warfare and parents abandoning them and expulsion from school and drug addiction. The people who were caring for these boys were doing a wonderful job, but sadly we heard a couple of months later there had been a tremendous fight between some of the children and they had succeeded in burning the whole place to the ground. The younger boys were taken to a place of safety and the older ones locked up.

Our final shoot that day was with the street gangs in the city, more sad tales, but I was surprised to see that many of them appeared quite happy. The gang leader had become the father figure they'd never had, and one way or another, they found enough to feed themselves and somewhere warm to sleep at night. Their biggest problem was glue sniffing. It was heartbreaking to know that few of them would ever survive to middle age. They would poison themselves long before that.

We made another programme for a furniture chain which was hoping its products would be accepted by Ikea, their target audience, and added to their range. Our clients hoped our video would really impress the Swedish company.

We spent several days touring the factories plus several furniture shops and I wanted to tear my hair out. Each time we tried to showcase a piece of furniture we were horrified at the bad workmanship. Doors hung askew, legs were wobbly and beds creaked when you sat on them.

I didn't realise it for several years but when furniture is assembled on the show room floor, screws, bolts and so on are not tightened, so it gives you the impression of bad workmanship. No one explained this to us at the time, and it took us many extra hours combing the shops to find good examples of furniture that didn't wobble or droop at an angle.

* * *

I met up with a colleague and friend from the old SABC days for coffee and I asked her why she looked so down.

"Do you realise," she said, "we should be lounging around in the Caribbean now, sunning ourselves and drinking piña coladas, without a care in the world?"

"However do you come up with that?"

"I'm just back from Los Angeles and the way they do things in America is so very different. They treat their scriptwriters with respect, *and* they pay them a decent amount of money too."

"Well we all know how mean the SABC are."

"That's not the point, it's the copyright side. Awkward Park (Auckland Park, the SABC head office) should never have got away with making us sign over all rights to our work. You know they sold on the 'Chickens' series to other countries in Africa?"

"Yes, and I was told they also sold the maths series, the English, and the science series, as far away as Nigeria."

"And we didn't receive another penny for any of it. In theory, we should be rolling in cash."

"I think they also sold on some of the radio programmes as well, recorded in English. But we knew what it was like, if we accepted the work, we had to sign away our copyright."

"Internationally, that's illegal," she told me.

"Yes, but only if the country is a signatory to the Berne Convention and South Africa never signed it." I had become wiser if not wealthier.

"No, apparently they signed something, but it was not ratified."

"Well either way, we were screwed."
Now we were both feeling down.

I worked in-house once more for the SABC, during the next round of national elections as they needed all the hands they could get. There were reporters and cameramen in every two-bit town and as the votes flooded in for the ANC, there were loud cheers and shrieks of joy. I had got to the stage that I didn't care who won as long as I could continue to get work and someone, somewhere could keep the crime levels under control.

I had always considered that working for National Geographic was the height of achievement for anyone in the industry, so I was thrilled when I was asked to post-script a programme from footage which had already been shot. It documented the story of a hand-reared honey badger on a game farm in Zimbabwe.

Honey badgers are considered among the fiercest animals in Africa, for while they may be small, they are incredibly aggressive and have been known to attack almost any animal when cornered, even chasing young lions from their kill. Their fur is loose, their skulls are extremely hard, and they are very difficult to kill. Once a honey badger takes hold of something it just does not let go. They can crack a tortoise shell, kill snakes and raid beehives. Bee stings, porcupine quills and animal bites rarely penetrate their skin, and if any creatures, even cattle, buffalos or large cats, intrude on their burrows, the honey badger will attack. They are quite tireless and will wear out their opponents.

It was a tremendous opportunity to be involved in the programme and besides writing the script, I worked with the editor to put all the footage together. Much of this had to be enhanced as the family who brought up the animal had shot it with a small domestic camera. Still, I am quite proud of the DVD in my cupboard, issued by National Geographic which bears my name on the back cover, even if it is in very tiny print and you have to squint to read it. I find a magnifying glass helpful.

This same award-winning production house which had recently moved to Durban was also engaged to compile a series for the BBC, relating the story of how the wildlife department were introducing lions into a game park where previously they had been absent. How were the other animals going to react, and how did the lions fare?

This was another exciting project and I wrote the script from the footage which had been provided and worked again with the same editor piecing it all together. We felt very pleased with our results and waited to receive lots of praise from London.

We didn't get it. They threw it back at us, saying it was too boring, they needed it hyped up. I honestly didn't understand what they wanted. Hyped up, like the commentary on a horse race? For wildlife? To me it didn't make sense. We did as we were told, but I wasn't happy with the result and it was only when I was living back in Europe that I understood what the producer wanted.

When I had watched wildlife documentaries, it was in the days of the calm, dulcet tones of David Attenborough, and I had no idea the format had changed. Now, everything is frenetic, possibly to appeal to a younger audience, but I am uncomfortable even watching programmes presented that way. I don't want to be fired up on the edge of my seat every moment the television is on. For sports, races and even game shows and competitions it makes sense but the same hype is not used in cooking programmes so why they should add animals to the 'will he or won't he survive?' genre I'm not sure. The whole production comes across as silly, especially when you realise how some of them are made.

Do you think that the same animals were shown all the time? Not always! Directors would have reams of footage of a particular species and its antics and then, in edit, could conjure up a story about a family and create their trials and tribulations and find suitable shots to show these. It wasn't all fake of course, but it wasn't uncommon. Today, with the success of spy cameras, we get more of the truth, and have you noticed it's not quite as dramatic?

There was also a change in attitudes, as I remembered from my days in Johannesburg. In one production house the people were tearing their hair out at having to re-make a wildlife programme because it showed a kill and there was lots of blood. The BBC wanted it sanitised in case it upset their more sensitive viewers.

But in South Africa the tide was turning, and it became harder and harder for me to get work. Admittedly I had undertaken many contracts for the provincial governments, and these were the first to follow the new regulations fostering the previously disadvantaged. I tried to get round this by asking black African friends to attend the tender meetings with the other two members of my crew, hoping they would give the correct answers. On another occasion I drove almost a hundred kilometres to hand deliver my tender document and post it in the correct box, only to learn that it was not there when the box was opened. I took that one as far as the ombudsman but got nowhere.

In the event, we were called in at the last minute, to salvage the project. The successful team had not shot sufficient footage, so we had to help edit and supply stock shots and recordings we had made in previous years.

There were other factors which prompted us to leave South Africa. Our maid was shot, yes with a gun, on our next door neighbour's front lawn. She was lucky to survive, but it was a nasty shock for all of us.

Also, we were not getting any younger and I was fast approaching pension age. My second husband and I had previously bought a holiday flat, or rather bolt-hole, in Spain, so this was to be our destination.

By now two of the children had settled in Australia and a third was on her way there shortly. We had no reason to stay in South Africa, except our deep love for the country and its people. The medical aid costs were also going through the roof, and we were rattling around in a house that was much too big for us. Did we really need three bathrooms and a massive pool we rarely used?

With four large suitcases and the dog in his travel box, we drove to Johannesburg and boarded a plane for Madrid.

A couple of years before, I had been writing a 'Weekly Letter from South Africa' which was broadcast on one of the local English language radio stations based in Alicante.

However by the time we landed, this had fallen away. I'd had it at the back of my mind that I could go on working, possibly on radio, but it didn't look hopeful.

For the first couple of months, retirement was fun. I got up when I pleased, I could linger over breakfast, finish the Sudoku and read as many books as I liked. But the euphoria did not last. Any kind of permanent work was going to be a problem with the language barrier, and there were plenty of people willing to work for free on the radio stations. I really should take a well deserved rest. I told myself I should relax and enjoy old age.

That worked for a while, but maybe writers are born and not made, because although it took a few months, it dawned on me that for the first time, I could write anything I wanted to. I wouldn't have a client screaming I'd got it all wrong. I could also make it as long or as short as I liked, I didn't have to judge the length of a script to the nearest second. I could also be my own publisher. I could maybe even write a book. But could I write a novel? There was only one way to find out. Sit down and write one. Then I thought that maybe I should write my biographies first, before I forgot some of the people I had met and places I had been. I got out the lap top.

It wasn't until I had moved back to Europe that the final award came in. I'd received many of these while I was working in Johannesburg and then again for the Durban Municipality, through the *National Television and Video Association*. Once I was operating under my own company, I never entered for any awards, most of the time I was too busy, and although they are nice to have, to be quite honest, those I have are still languishing in a box under the bed. (I no longer have the luxury of a study where I can hang them on the wall). When you are self-employed your priority is work, and a steady stream of it. Awards may be nice but they don't pay the bills.

I had an unexpected call from Durban Water Department to say they had won the '*United Nations Decade of Water Award*', and since I had written and produced nearly all the videos, written many of the brochures, designed their conference posters and also helped with their corporate displays, both nationally and internationally, would I like to go to Zaragoza and attend the award ceremony? Do fish swim in water? Of course I wanted to go!

The Water Department worked hand in hand with Sanitation and Waste, and I saw plenty of waste in my time with the Durban Council. I was always impressed with the new innovations they were introducing. They experimented with every new piece of technology that came on the market, to bring basic services to the masses which crowded into the informal settlements around Durban. If I had climbed around one kind of toilet system I had crawled around them all. As each type was assessed for practicality, acceptance and viability, they adapted each prototype one after the other. If any department deserved an award it was Durban Water.

I was a little worried as to what to wear, as we had seriously, and I mean seriously, downsized when we moved from South Africa to Spain. Remember, only nineteen, medium-sized cardboard boxes which were even smaller than the four large suitcases we took on the plane. Yes, it's quite true.

I had no idea how the Spanish celebrated such award ceremonies but with the United Nations also involved, didn't they always have money to throw around like it was going out of fashion?

I packed my remaining evening dress, and test squeezed my 'other half' into his tuxedo. Maybe we wouldn't look too bad. We packed up the car and off we drove to Zaragoza, where our evening clothes remained at the bottom of the suitcases.

What a difference! A short, formal ceremony held in what I think was the City Hall, a couple of videos, and how I itched to re-edit, even re-shoot the one shown by the United Nations, a few short speeches, and we were out of there! The mayor entertained us to a brilliant lunch downstairs in the oldest tapas bar in the city, and then we were treated to a walk around the main streets of the old town. Finally we took a ride around the huge exhibition park they'd built for one of the large expos held in the city.

This was a stark contrast to the gala banquets, the top performing acts from Cape Town and Johannesburg, and the dozens of speeches from premiers, mayors, sponsors and anyone else who could get a look in. Maybe the United Nations did not have buckets of money to throw around after all.

From the videos I had watched at the UN award ceremony, and from some of the programmes I had watched beamed over from British television, our industry in South Africa had nothing to be ashamed of. There is always a hierarchy in any work culture with those ensconced in head office at the top of the tree, and those in the provinces and small towns lower down the totem pole.

Johannesburg people looked down on those who made programmes in Durban, but they were all looked down on by Britain and America as being at the bottom of the bigger tree. This is partly understandable as South Africa didn't have a television service until 1976, and went on air in colour from the beginning, but their first dramas were overacted by artists who had transferred directly from the stage and used the same techniques, which do not work on television.

A couple of decades on, their programming ranked among the best in the world, especially their advertisements which have won many international awards.

And so, as we travelled the length and breadth of South Africa, we were treated like royalty. We saw traditional games and dancing, libraries in shipping containers, women employed to weed the roadsides, posh game lodges in Kruger Park, small business incubators, street children shelters, consumer affairs complaints divisions, dictionaries to interpret the slang used by the street children, and education initiatives. There were cholera prevention campaigns, population and demographic projects, museums, food security programmes, job creation groups, tourism promotion, and educational demonstrations.

Some were working, others were not as successful, but in all but a couple of cases, there were people working with passion, commitment and boundless energy to improve the lives of other people. This, for me, came at a time when everyone else was grumbling about South

Africa going downhill, systems falling apart, and crime and corruption on the rise. I clung to the belief that I had seen the other side of the coin and it gave me hope for the country I had come to love.

I have been so extremely lucky to have worked for so many years where I jumped out of bed in the morning and cried "Yes! It's Monday!" It was not easy to think of it as work when I enjoyed so much of it, except that I was exhausted at the end of each day. Even sitting in an edit suite and concentrating on those small screens can be tiring, and perhaps editors and producer directors watch less television than most people, as the last thing they want to do when they get home is look at another small screen all evening!

Making any kind of insert, short programme, series, or Hollywood blockbuster, is the result of teamwork, and even at my humble level I could never have produced anything at all without the hard work and dedication of all the people who helped me to make it all possible. I cannot thank those crew members enough, you know who you are, even if I have changed a few names. I owe so much too to all those people who had enough faith in me to ask me to make their programmes.

Thank you too, to those hundreds, possibly thousands, of people who helped us to show their problems and their successes by role playing so many scenes and sharing their lives with us for a day or two. The lollipops, buckets and bowls are long gone, but somewhere in dark dusty cupboards, lie the visual memories of the day you helped us show how you lived.

I feel very honoured to have been given the opportunity to see so much of Africa far, far away from the major cities, welcomed into people's homes, fed and watered, given presents and hugs and made to feel part of the family.

I met so many interesting characters with really interesting stories to tell, and I was proud to help them document and broadcast their experiences. This world is full of people who are trying to make a difference and while the media leaps onto every dismal story with alacrity, it was a privilege to be on the positive side.

If just one life has been improved by one of our programmes about simple things like washing hands, using toilets, rehydrating those who are ill, preparing food hygienically, setting up a business, or any of the other topics we covered, then it will all have been worthwhile and we too will have helped to make a difference.

And what about Caroline? How did I kill her? I transported her to Africa and pegged her out firmly on the ground. She was eventually devoured by fire ants, a particularly nasty way to die. Maybe one day I'll write about why she deserved such a painful death!

THE END

ABOUT THE AUTHOR

Lucinda E Clarke has been a professional writer for the last 30 years, scripting for both radio and television. She's had numerous articles published in several magazines and currently writes a monthly column in a local publication. She once had her own newspaper column, until the newspaper closed down, but says this was not her fault!

She has won over 20 awards for scripting, directing, concept and producing, and had two educational textbooks published. Sadly these did not make her the fortune she dreamed of, to allow her to live in the manner to which she would like to be accustomed.

Lucinda has also worked as an announcer on radio (on one occasion with a bayonet at her throat) appeared on television, and met and interviewed some of the world's top leaders.

She set up and ran her own video production company, making a variety of programmes, from advertisements to corporate to drama documentaries on a vast range of subjects. Altogether she has lived in eight different countries, run the 'worst riding school in the world', and cleaned toilets to bring the money in.

When she handled her own divorce, Lucinda made legal history in South Africa.

She gives occasional talks and lectures to special interest groups and finds retirement the most exhausting time of her life so far but says there is still so much to see and do, she is worried she won't have time to fit it all in.

© Lucinda E Clarke 2020

TO MY READERS

I hope you have enjoyed reading this book (or even if you didn't like it), please would you take a few minutes to write a review? Reviews are very important to authors and I would certainly value your feedback. Thank you.

Connect with Lucinda E Clarke:
On Facebook
https://www.facebook.com/lucindaeclarke.author
By emaillucindaeclarke@gmail.com
Bloghttp://lucindaeclarke.wordpress.com
Twitter   @LucindaEClarke

ALSO BY LUCINDA E CLARKE

A Year in the life of Leah Brand
The nightmare began the day the dog died. Leah's cosy new world is turned upside down as inanimate objects move around the house on their own, there are unexplained noises, and slowly she is driven to the edge of madness.

A Year in the life of Andrea Coe

Andrea Coe was Leah's best friend; she was outgoing, outrageous and the opposite of quiet and shy Leah. What as the attraction? And is Andrea's friendship genuine? How well do we know our friends?

Walking over Eggshells

The first autobiography which relates Lucinda's horrendous relationship with her mother and her travels to various countries.

The *very* Worst Riding School in the World (free)

Who in their right mind would open and run a riding school when they can't ride, are terrified of horses, with no idea of how to care for them and no insurance or capital? Add to that two of the four horses are not fit for the knacker's yard. Yes, that would be me.

Truth, Lies and Propaganda

The first of two books explaining how Lucinda 'fell' into writing for a living – her dream since childhood. It began when she was fired from her teaching job, and crashed out in an audition at the South African Broadcasting Corporation. In a quirky turn of fate, she found herself writing a series on how to care for domestic livestock, she knew absolutely nothing about cows, goats and chickens. And it all continued from there.

More Truth, Lies and Propaganda

Tales of filming in deep rural Africa, meeting a ram with an identity crisis, a house that disappears, the forlorn bushmen and a video starring a very dead rat. You will never believe anything you watch on television ever again.

Amie - African Adventure

A novel set in Africa, which takes Amie from the comfort of her home in England to a small African country. Civil war breaks out and soon she is fighting for her life.

Amie and the Child of Africa

As Amie goes in search of the child she fostered before the civil war broke out, she encounters a terrorist organization with international connections. She is not alone, but one of her friends will betray her.

Amie Stolen Future

In one night, Amie loses everything, her home, her family, her possessions and her name. She has nowhere to turn, but she has no freedom for other people now control her life and if she does not obey them, they will not let her live.

Amie Cut for Life

A look and listen mission turns out to be a nightmare as Amie is left to rescue four young girls who are destined for the sex slave trade with a horrifying twist.

Samantha (Amie backstory 1)

A light comedy as Amie's sister ventures overseas for the first time with her boyfriend Gerry – if it can go wrong, it goes wrong.

Ben (Amie backstory 2)

Ben's story of his passage into manhood and the beginning of the civil war in Togodo.

Unhappily Ever After

The real truth you've never been told before. In Fairyland, Cinderella is scheming to get a divorce with a good settlement from King Charming, and the other royal marriages are also in dire trouble. This year's ball is approaching, along with a political agitator hell bent on rousing the peasants into revolting against their royal masters.

A YEAR

In The Life of

LEAH BRAND

LUCINDA E CLARKE

JANUARY LEAH

The nightmare began on the day the dog died.

It was New Year's Eve and, while Mason and I were out celebrating, my nemesis passed on to the big kennel in the sky. By the time we struggled out of the taxi, neither of us was in a fit state to notice the dog, dead or alive. Mason had to grab my arm as I caught my foot in the door jamb on the way out of the Uber. It was just as well the price of the fare would be billed automatically on the credit card; Mason was not sober enough to find the right notes to pay the driver.

We weaved our way up the path, arms linked, concentrating hard trying not to fall. It felt a long, long way to the front door. Mason propped me against the wall and then looked at me.

"Keys," he barked.

"I don't have them." Despite the pain above my left knee I couldn't stop myself from giggling. "Look in your pockets."

"I gave them to you." The fluorescent light from the lamp post on the street near the gate illuminated the scowl on Mason's face.

"No, you didn't," I replied, but to placate him I fumbled with the clasp on my dinky evening bag as if to check. The problem was I needed both hands to undo the clasp and I swayed from side to side desperately trying to keep my balance. I didn't remember drinking all that much, but I couldn't even stand straight and I knew before I peered into my purse it only contained a small wad of paper hankies and a lipstick.

"I don't have them," I repeated.

Mason glared at me and began digging into the pockets of his dinner suit. He cursed loudly.

"Hush, you'll wake the neighbours!" Apart from Andrea we didn't know any of them all that well, but I often got the uncomfortable feeling they did not approve of us. Well maybe that was a bit harsh, but I'd tried to get to know them and had little luck.

"To hell with the neighbours," Mason shouted louder. "Happy New Year," he screamed. "Stuffy lot, in bed already? Night to celebrate! It's a brand New Year."

I grabbed his arm, as much to steady myself as to quieten him down. The pains continued to shoot up and down the leg that was no longer there as I made a valiant attempt to stay upright. I had a moment of clarity. "The spare key, it's under the middle flowerpot, over there." I pointed to the row of them arranged next to the step under the lounge window.

Mason staggered back, bent down and put his hand out as his legs gave way and he promptly fell over. He looked so comical lying there. The well-respected owner and head of the biggest law firm in town sprawled on the grass. Then I really got a fit of the giggles and laughed until the tears ran down my face.

One look at Mason's face helped sober me up. He did not appreciate anyone making fun of him. He took his dignity and his professional standing in the community very seriously. He turned his attention back to the flowerpots, lifting each in turn until he found the key.

"Yes!" He slipped the ring over his finger and twirled it around and I watched in horror as it flew off and landed in the holly bush halfway down the path.

The holly bush fought back, tearing at Mason's hands as he fumbled among the leaves to retrieve it. There were several futile attempts to insert it in the lock after which we both tumbled into the hall. Next hurdle was to navigate the stairs, fling open the bedroom door and collapse on the bed.

It took me a while to orientate myself as the ceiling revolved above me. Good heavens, how much wine had I drunk? I manoeuvred my way towards our bathroom by clinging onto the furniture. I tore off my black evening gown and my prosthesis, and hopped into the shower. I leaned against the wall and let the steaming water pour over me before I realised I was still wearing my bra and panties. But I was past caring. I think, if I remember correctly, I was beginning to sober up and questioning why I was this far out of it after less than half a bottle of wine. I don't drink all that often; I'd got out of the habit while taking the cocktail of drugs they poured into me after the accident. Everyone knows medicine and alcohol can be lethal. Now, I was down to a few daily tablets but I'd not taken any for a couple of days beforehand. I knew there would be plenty of booze at the party but maybe even the modest amount I had was enough to make me really drunk.

I clutched the shower door, grabbed a towel, sat on the loo and rubbed myself hard all over. My head was pounding but the biggest pain was in my leg, the one that wasn't there. How could my brain be so stupid? Consciously I knew the surgeons who saved my life had no option but to remove a limb crushed beyond repair. Five years later some of those complicated synapses told me it was still there and throbbing. I should take some of my pills but they were downstairs and I would never make it in my condition. I hopped back into the bedroom where Mason was comatose, spread corner to corner across the bed, arms akimbo, his dinner jacket crumpled and stained and his shoes covered in mud. He was out for the count.

I sighed. I knew that nothing short of a nuclear explosion would wake him, so I sank onto the bed, removed his shoes and rolled him over to his side. I pulled out my nightie from under the pillow and slipped it over my head, crawled under the duvet and, despite the pain, I remembered no more.

Loud, piercing shrieks coming from downstairs woke me. I flung myself out of bed, and tumbled onto the floor. In moments of stress I still forgot I can't walk. Swearing under my breath I rubbed my eyes and grabbed my false leg. Strapping it on, I dragged on my dressing gown and opened the bedroom door. It was no use trying to wake Mason; he was still dead to the world and not even the cries from below would wake him. I hurried down the stairs as quickly as I could. I knew who was screaming but I didn't know why.

Belinda was standing in the kitchen, still shrieking, when I shuffled in.

"What's the problem? Stop it. Calm down." A quick glance showed everything looked normal. The back door was still closed, the window panes intact, the counter tops as clean and tidy as I'd left them before going out last night. Everything in place, if you ignored the spilled cereal all over the floor where Belinda had dropped the corn flakes. They crunched under my feet as I went to hold her but she stepped quickly out of reach and backed up against the pantry door. She looked petrified.

*   *   *

A YEAR

In The Life of

ANDREA COE

LUCINDA E CLARKE